a practical guide to

FINANCIAL MANAGEMENT

FOR charities AND voluntary

organisations

▼ KATE SAYER ▼

DIRECTORY OF SOCIAL CHANGE

Published by
The Directory of Social Change
24 Stephenson Way
London NW1 2DP
Tel: 020 7209 5151, fax: 020 7391 4804
e-mail: books@dsc.org.uk
from whom further copies and a full publications list are available.
In association with Sayer Vincent
8 Angel Gate, City Road, London EC1V 2SJ Tel: 020 7841 6360
e-mail: info@sayervincent.co.uk

The Directory of Social Change is Registered Charity no. 800517

First edition published 1998
Second edition published 2002

ISBN 1 903991 29 3

British Library Cataloguing in Publication Data
A catalogue record for this book is available from the British Library

Cover design by Penny Drinkwater
Designed and typeset by Kate Bass
Printed and bound by Page Bros., Norwich

Directory of Social Change London Office:
Courses and Conferences tel: 020 7209 4949
Charityfair tel: 020 7209 1015
Publicity tel: 020 7391 4900
Research tel: 020 7391 4880
Charity Centre tel: 020 7209 1015

Directory of Social Change Liverpool Office:
Federation House, Hope Street, Liverpool L1 9BW
Courses and Conferences tel: 0151 708 0117
Research tel: 0151 708 0136

CONTENTS

SECTION 1

FINANCIAL MANAGEMENT AND PLANNING

SECTION 2

ACCOUNTS AND AUDIT

SECTION 3

TAX AND VAT

GLOSSARY OF TERMS

Accountant's Report

A report by a qualified accountant on the annual accounts confirming that the accounts have been properly prepared. It is instead of an audit and only available to smaller charitable companies with gross income below £250,000. Also known as a compilation report.

Accruals Basis

This is a method of accounting which adjusts the receipts and payments for amounts which should have been collected or paid before the end of the accounting period, in order to arrive at the income and expenditure account.

Assets

Assets are the money, goods and property which an organisation possesses, including any legal rights it may have to receive money, goods, services and property from others.

Balance Sheet

A summary of the assets and liabilities of an organisation at a particular date. Sometimes described as a 'snapshot' of an organisation. It also describes the funds which are represented by the net assets.

Capital Budget

This is the plan for large-scale expenditure on building or equipment; together with the funding plan.

Capital

The capital of a charity is a restricted fund (or funds) which the trustees must retain for the benefit of the charity and not spend. A capital fund is also known as an endowment fund.

Capitalisation

When property or equipment is purchased and treated as an asset on the balance sheet, it is said to be capitalised. This means that the cost is not treated as an operating cost and is not charged to the expense accounts.

Charitable Expenditure

This comprises all expenditure relating to the objects of the charity. It includes grants payable, the cost of supporting charitable activities and projects and management and administration of the charity.

Compilation Report

A report by a qualified accountant on the annual accounts confirming that the accounts have been properly prepared. It is instead of an audit and only available to smaller charitable companies with gross income below £250,000.

Creditors

The amounts owed by an organisation to others; included in liabilities.

Debtors

The amounts owed to the organisation for goods or services supplied. 'Aged debtors' is a break-down of the total owed to the organisation month by month.

Depreciation

An allowance for wear and tear made on long-lasting property and equipment. An amount charged annually as an expense to spread the cost of fixed assets over their useful economic life.

Designated Funds

Designated funds are unrestricted funds which have been earmarked for a particular purpose by the trustees.

Endowment

An endowment is a special type of restricted fund which must be retained intact and not spent.

Expendable Endowment

This is a type of endowment fund where trustees have the discretion to eventually convert the fund into expendable income.

Financial Reporting Standard

This is a statement of required good practice for all company accounts and all accounts which purport to give a true and fair view. It is obligatory for all published accounts to comply with Financial Reporting Standards. They are issued by a committee of accounting bodies and cover a range of accounting topics, with updated versions issued regularly.

Financial Statements

The accounts of an organisation including the notes to the accounts and any other statements which are required to be included.

Fixed Assets

These are assets which continue to be of value to the organisation year after year and which the trustees hold on a long term basis and therefore do not intend to dispose of in the short term.

Fundraising and Publicity Costs

These are costs of obtaining funds for the charity's work, such as advertising, direct mail, staff time, agent's fees.

General Funds

These are unrestricted funds which have not been earmarked and may be used generally to further the charity's stated objects.

Governing Document

This is the document which establishes the charity and has to be passed by the Charity Commission prior to registration of the charity. It sets out the charity's objects and the rules of the organisation. It may be known by several different names: governing instrument; constitution; trust deed; Memorandum and Articles of Association (for a charitable company); Rules (for an Industrial and Provident Society); explanatory document (in Scotland); founding deed (in Scotland).

Gross Income

Generally means all the income of an organisation for the financial year before deductions of any expenses. Specifically defined for the purposes of thresholds under the Charities Act to exclude all capital (endowment) incoming resources, sale of fixed assets, and sale of investments.

Impairment

This is the term used to describe a fall in value of an asset. An impairment review may be required for certain tangible fixed assets. This is usually when some major event has occurred which causes you to think that the previous values ascribed to the asset are no longer valid.

Income and Expenditure Account

A summary of the income due and expenditure incurred for a financial year, showing the revenue transactions only.

Incoming Resources

All resources available to a charity, including incoming capital (endowment), restricted income, gifts in kind and intangible income.

Independent Examination

Charities with gross income and total expenditure not exceeding £250,000 may have an independent examination instead of an audit. This is a type of external examination brought in by the Charities Act 1993 which ay be undertaken by anyone with some experience of accounting, but who does not have to be a qualified accountant or auditor. Detailed guidance on the independent examination has been issued by the Charity Commission.

Liabilities

Liabilities are the amounts owed by an organisation at the balance sheet date. The cost will already have been incurred, but the bill not paid.

Management and Administration

These are the costs incurred in the management of the charity's assets, organisational administration and statutory requirements.

Net Book Value

The net book value is calculated for tangible fixed assets by taking the original cost or valuation amount and deducting the accumulated depreciation. The net book value is the amount at which tangible fixed assets are stated in the balance sheet.

Nominal Ledger

The nominal ledger is the summary of transactions, drawing together all the basic entries.

Permanent Endowment

This is a type of endowment fund where the trustees must retain the fund intact as capital and use the funds to generate income or hold the assets (depending on the terms of the trust). The trustees have no discretion to convert the endowment into expendable income.

Receipts and Payments Account

A simple form of accounts which summarises the cash transactions of a charity. An option available to smaller charities.

Registered Auditor

An accountant or firm of accountants registered to undertake company audits and are regulated in their work by one of the accountancy bodies.

Restricted Fund

This is a fund subject to specific trusts within the objects of the charity (e.g. by a letter from the donor at the time of the gift, or by the terms of a public appeal). It may be a capital fund, which cannot be spent but must be retained for the benefit of the charity, or it may be an income fund, which must be spent on the specified purpose within a reasonable time.

Scottish Charity

A body established in Scotland and recognised as charitable by the Inland Revenue.

SORP

(see Statement of Recommended Practice)

Statement of Assets and Liabilities

A summary required for charities preparing accounts under the receipts and payments basis. Not the same as a balance sheet; non-monetary assets do not have to be valued.

Statement of Financial Activities

Abbreviated to SoFA. Financial statement introduced especially for charities in the SORP. Summarises all incoming resources and application of resources. Replaces the income and expenditure account as a primary financial statement, it goes further by bringing together all the transactions of a charity.

Statement of Recommended Practice

Guidance on the appropriate treatment of items in the accounts of specialised bodies.

Stock

The value of goods on hand at the balance sheet date will be included in stock under current assets.

Support Costs

These are part of the direct charitable expenditure and may be the management of projects from a central office. They may include a fair proportion of central office running costs.

Tangible Fixed Assets

Long-term assets that have some substance, such as buildings and equipment.

Total Expenditure

All the outgoings of an organisation for a financial year, excluding purchases of fixed assets and investments.

Unrestricted Funds

These are funds held for the general purposes of the charity, to be spent within the stated objects.

INTRODUCTION

Financial management is about good stewardship of the assets available to a charity, as well as ensuring that the organisation has the resources it needs to fulfil its objects and plans. The legal responsibility for the good financial management of a charity ultimately rests with the trustees, although in larger charities paid staff will have a significant role to play.

Financial management is part of management as a whole and should not be seen as a separate activity left entirely to accountants or the finance department. This book is addressed largely to those without an accounting background and aims to equip them with the basic knowledge and skills they need to exercise good financial management practices. It is only a starting point however, and managers will need to enhance their skills and develop good financial management practice through experience.

Although written for charities, the book will also be relevant to voluntary and other non-profit-making organisations that are not registered charities. The principles of good financial management apply to all these organisations and most will have a management structure similar to charities.

The first few chapters cover the basics of financial planning, including tasks such as costing, drawing up a budget, monitoring cashflow, managing risk, and presenting and using financial information to make decisions. The second section covers the actual production and interpretation of accounts, including basic bookkeeping, preparing annual accounts, the Charity Commission's Statement of Recommended Practice (SORP), and annual auditing requirements. These sections have been updated in the second edition for the revised charity SORP issued in October 2000, as well as the revised Accounts and Reports Regulations 2000. However, these sections are examined in greater depth in a new volume in the series *A Practical Guide to Charity Accounting*, to be published in 2003. Those who are familiar with this area may wish to skip these chapters. However, I am aware that many accountants and managers new to the charity sector may be looking for guidance on these issues.

The financial management of charities must be understood against the appropriate legal background. Charities are affected by many different laws in addition to charity law, and some reference is made to these as appropriate. Tax laws affect charities in specific ways, and so chapters have been devoted to trading and VAT in the final section of the book. The second edition includes a completely re-written Chapter 11 to reflect the major changes to Gift aid and other forms of tax-effective giving. All chapters have been updated to reflect the law up to May 2002.

This book does not aim to be comprehensive and so the Further Reading section at the end lists other books which cover relevant and related areas – such as employment law – in more depth. In addition, regular updated information is available on the Sayer Vincent website www.sayervincent.co.uk

Kate Sayer is a chartered accountant with over 18 years' experience of the charity and not-for-profit sector. She is a partner with Sayer Vincent, a specialist consultancy focussing on IT, audit, governance and financial management issues for charities and not-for-profit organisations.

Sayer Vincent
8 Angel Gate
City Road
London
EC1V 2SJ

Tel: 020 7841 6360

E-mail: info@sayervincent.co.uk

Website: www.sayervincent.co.uk

SECTION 1

FINANCIAL MANAGEMENT AND PLANNING

Chapter 1

FINANCIAL PLANNING

THE PLANNING CYCLE

Financial planning does not start with numbers. In fact, it is impossible to just start a financial forecast without some idea of what you want to do and how. Good budgets can only be produced as a result of good underlying financial plans. Since there are always a number of variable factors, there may be considerable changes over the life of such a plan. It is appropriate to think of the whole process as a cycle, because you have to review plans and budgets all the time.

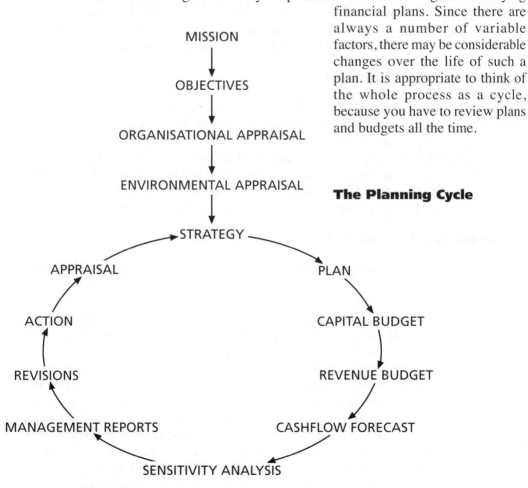

The Planning Cycle

Mission

Most organisations have a mission statement. In fact, charities and voluntary organisations have always been fairly clear about their objectives, because these have to be established in order to set the charity up. Charities are motivated by a cause and this is usually well-known to staff, volunteers and trustees. However the process of drawing up a mission statement that focuses and clarifies the purposes of the organisation can be very beneficial.

Objectives

Whilst the overall mission of the charity may be obvious, the objectives for the medium term will need careful thought. Objectives will often be the building bricks that will help the organisation achieve its mission. For example, an objective might be the creation of a national service from a current base of one or two localities. Or a charity might decide that its objective is to offer a place on an IT training course for every young person in their area of operation. At this stage of the planning process the objectives may be stated in fairly general terms, but should give focus to the organisation's work. The organisation may decide on some specifically financial objectives, such as achieving a certain level of general reserves.

Organisational Appraisal

Having decided on the general direction the organisation will take over the next few years, it will need to assess its strengths and weaknesses in relation to its objectives. This process may identify new skills and additional resources that will be needed, which could include staff, or new premises, or new computer equipment. Identifying strengths and weaknesses will help the organisation to decide on the overall timetable for achieving its aims. It may decide to build on strengths first, and address the weaknesses later.

Environmental Appraisal

Just as commercial undertakings need to assess the market need for their goods or services, charities should assess the need for their work. Charities need concrete information about their particular 'market', which may come from publicly available statistics, research, or information gathered by the charity itself. This part of the planning process should also consider the organisation's competitors: who else is providing a similar service or meeting the same need? This will be essential when putting together fundraising plans, as any potential funder will expect answers to these types of questions. The organisation should focus on the opportunities and threats presented by external forces. The outcome of this part of the work may be to identify the constraining factors, such as other charities working in the field, the potential withdrawal of government funding, the actual number of potential beneficiaries, difficulty recruiting suitably trained staff and so on. These constraining factors will all need to be fed into the financial plans.

Strategy

The strategy tries to set out the overall approach the organisation is going to take to get from A to B, where A is where the organisation is now and B is where it wants to be in so many years time, as expressed in the objectives. So, if one of the objectives is to become a national charity, the strategy should set out the actions needed to achieve this outcome.

Plan

The strategy may be sub-divided into several, more specific and detailed plans. So there may be a fundraising plan, an IT plan, a staffing plan and so on. The financial plan will be included here. Whilst the Objectives and Strategy should be established at the beginning of the planning cycle and remain more or less the same for a long period of time, the plans will need to be reviewed and refined as progress is made. For example, the strategy may remain the same, but the timescale in which it can be achieved may have to be reviewed again and again. Plans describe the short-term activities of the organisation, looking about one year ahead.

Capital Budget

In accounting terms, capital refers to large, one-off expenditure on items such as equipment, property or other fixed assets. The capital budget will be the plan for acquiring new fixed assets and how they will be funded. It needs to look about five years ahead, although changes may well be necessary as you go forward. Usually the timing changes, rather than the overall budget. The capital budget will dovetail in with other plans; for example the IT plan will probably lead to a plan for acquisition of computers and equipment. Notes to explain the figures in the budget are essential. The implications for revenue budgets and cashflow should be noted for incorporation into those forecasts. For example, the maintenance for new equipment should be incorporated into the revenue budget.

Revenue Budget

The revenue budget is the working budget for the organisation and covers the running costs and any projects. It is usually referred to simply as 'the budget' of an organisation because it relates to daily operations. The revenue budget is built up from the detailed plans for staffing, fundraising, IT and other operational areas. Its purpose is to see how the pieces of the jigsaw fit together. Incoming resources have to match the spending plans; the spending plans have to reflect the best use of resources. Revenue budgets should be prepared in detail for the year ahead, but in outline for several years beyond. They may have to be changed many times, but it is important that the organisation has some feel for the financial implications of the objectives and plans. Assumptions will have to be made in preparing the revenue budgets and so these should be written down and kept for future reference.

Cashflow Forecast

The cashflow forecast will be based on the detailed plans, the revenue budget and the capital budget. What this will show is whether the organisation will have the cash resources to meet the needs of the plans within the agreed timetable. If the plan requires expansion and spending first, with additional incoming resources later, this will be a strain on cash resources. The working capital needs of the organisation will be identified in the cashflow forecast.

Sensitivity Analysis

This technique needs to be applied to the most uncertain elements in your budgets and forecasts. You should calculate the effects of changes to test your financial plans for robustness. For example, 'What if staff pay goes up by 7% instead of 4%'? Can the organisation pass on the increase to purchasers of their services? Can the organisation absorb the extra cost? Can costs be cut elsewhere? This exercise may enable the organisation to prepare a certain number of contingency plans or different options they can switch to depending on events.

Financial Reports

Financial reports should be comparisons to the agreed budgets, so that performance can be measured. The notes on assumptions will be needed, to help ascertain what elements of the plans did not happen as expected.

Revisions

Revisions follow on naturally from the reporting, as part of the cycle is the learning process. Plans improve as the organisation gets better at reading the information available.

Action

An important part of the planning cycle for a voluntary organisation is securing the trustees' approval of the plans. This gives staff a mandate to get on with the work in the plan and implicit approval to spend funds in accordance with the plans and budgets. Authorisation may still be needed for certain actions, but clearly agreed plans and budgets will help the organisation to take action immediately.

Appraisal

This means an appraisal for the whole organisation, not just of individual plans. You also need to assess the planning process to see how well it worked. For example, does the budgeting process work for trustees and staff? Appraisal also means that you have to set performance indicators at the beginning of the planning cycle in order to measure the success of a plan.

Summary

The whole planning process is a cycle, and in reality you never stop planning. Plans have to be a live part of what the organisation is doing. You do not need to rewrite them every five minutes, as the written version is only one part of the process. The activity of planning and having a planning framework is important for an organisation to be responsive and able to cope with change. Such organisations are usually more successful at their fundraising, as the planning framework is apparent in all their dealings with potential funders. It does take some time to develop a planning process that involves people and works for your organisation. That should not put you off. You do not have to be perfect at planning before you can start. The most important thing is to start. Then you can improve!

The rest of this chapter will look at practical ways in which you can draw together elements of a plan, concentrating on the financial aspects. Different elements will have greater or lesser importance for different organisations, but the formats and techniques described below should give you some templates you can use as appropriate for your situation.

COSTING

In order to budget properly you need to understand how costs arise and what affects them. Figures in budgets or accounts really are meaningless unless they can be put into a context. You will not draw up a good revenue budget for next year by taking last year's accounts or last year's budget and adding 5% to everything.

Example

In last year's accounts the amount for staff costs for the year was £154,896, including employer's national insurance. You estimate that the pay rise will be 5% and so want to put £162,641 into the revenue budget, to reflect a 5% increase on last year's accounts figure. This will be inaccurate because included in that accounts figure were the effects of:

◆ one staff member leaving half way through the year, and the replacement starting one month before the year end

◆ one staff member being on maternity leave for three months of the year, with no cover through staff costs budget. Agency staff have been used, but this is in the budget for relief staff.

You also know that one member of staff will be retiring half way through the coming year and there are no plans to replace him. Drawing up a more detailed plan of staff who will be in post for the coming year, you also realise that some staff are due increments and others are already at the top of the scale. In addition, the pay increase comes half way through the year. A more detailed calculation reveals that the budget ought to be £155,000 – about the same as last year's expenditure.

Staff costs often represent a major proportion of a voluntary organisation's expenditure and so it pays to spend some time on the build up of that item. You will also need to look at how your organisation treats expenditure such as temporary cover. Other expenditure items will not necessarily involve so much effort. For example, if you have a photocopier lease and repayments are fixed over the term of the lease, there is no need to add 5% to last year's accounting figure for the next year's budget. The approach 'add x% onto all expenditure headings' will produce inaccurate budgets, which means that they will probably be ignored, rather than used as a management tool. Even if you are a grant funded group and you know that your funding is going to increase (or decrease) by a fixed percentage, you cannot prepare a useful expenditure budget by simply marking up existing headings by a fixed percentage.

So it is a good idea to understand more about the costs in the organisation. By looking at historic information and investigating the basis of the amounts shown in financial accounts, you will learn about the types of costs, what makes them increase or decrease and how predictable they are.

Reviewing the Past – Checklist

The following questions may assist in gathering relevant information, but the list can be extended if necessary.

1. How many members did the organisation have last year? How many sites did we cover? What services did we provide and to what extent?

2. How many staff did we employ? Check on part-time or staff only employed for part of the year. What posts did they fill and were there vacancies during the year?

3. What salary scales are applied?

4. How did we account for temporary or relief staff?

5. How many volunteers did we have and what work did they do?

6. Were there any one-off expenses which will not apply again? (e.g. cost of moving to new premises)

7. How much do our premises cost us to run? Are there any factors which will change that? (e.g. rent reviews)

8. Which costs particularly related to certain projects? (e.g. cost of printing a report relating to a funded project)

9. Are there any projects which are time-limited? Are the costs of these separately identified?

10. Are there any particular policy decisions which affect our expenditure? (e.g. training policy, policy for charging fees)

11. What is the state of our equipment (fixed assets) and how has this been funded in the past?

12. Do we have on-going commitments? (e.g. photocopier lease)

New Organisations

If you are setting up a new organisation, think about the activities you will be undertaking and start a list of cost headings without making any attempt at this stage to put a figure beside them. You can do the research later to get estimates of the costs.

Analysing Costs

Variable and Fixed Costs

Once you have identified the main areas of spending for your organisation, you should be able to divide the spending into variable and fixed costs.

◆ Variable costs vary in proportion to the level of activity of the organisation.
◆ Fixed costs are usually the overheads of an organisation or department and are the costs incurred regardless of the level of activity. It does not mean that the actual amount in the budget is fixed; it means that the volume needed does not vary greatly, even though the price may vary. So, for example, you would need the same amount of heating in a building regardless of the number of projects being run from it.

Direct and Indirect Costs

Classifying the costs as direct or indirect is another way of looking at them in relation to the structure of the organisation and the department in which the costs arise. Larger charities tend to have departmental structures – there will be a number of projects, often self-financing, and a central administration department which usually has little income of its own.

◆ Direct costs are those directly attributable to a particular project or department.
◆ Indirect costs are those that relate to the organisation as a whole. Central administration costs are indirect costs since they cover all projects but generally do not relate specifically to any one.

Understanding Costs

Both these methods of analysing costs can be relevant at the same time. Variable costs tend also to be direct costs, but not always. Variable or fixed is a question of how the costs behave in relation to the level of activity; direct or indirect is a question of where the cost arises.

Looking at your list of cost headings, can you analyse them into the different types of costs?

◆ Is it a cost the organisation incurs regardless of activities or funding? e.g. lease commitments, rent and insurance on premises (fixed cost)?
◆ Is it a cost only arising because you plan to undertake a certain activity? e.g. hall hire for an event (direct cost)?
◆ Is it a cost which increases when you expand the organisation? e.g. staff travel, staff training (direct cost – dependent on number of staff)?
◆ Is it a cost which varies to some extent, but has a core cost which is unavoidable? e.g. telephone – the rental costs and a few calls are inevitable, but extra activity does push up the calls costs (mixed cost).

Understanding your costs will help you to make more accurate forecasts, and also to interpret management accounts and reports. Fixed costs are generally unavoidable costs, in the short term at least. It is usually easiest to group these together (for example all premises costs) and the budget estimates can probably be prepared without a great deal of effort. Because these costs are unavoidable, there should not be a lot of time spent by staff and trustees discussing them. The notes to the budget should explain the basis for the estimates in the budget and so any major mistakes will be picked up.

Contribution Analysis

Once you have identified the cost headings which are likely to be your fixed costs, you should be able to use this information to draw a picture of the overall cost structure of the organisation. The total of the fixed costs of the organisation is the amount of contribution needed from income-earning projects, grants and other activities in order for the organisation to break even. These activities have to cover their direct costs as well, so this is not the same as the total income needed for a particular project.

EXAMPLE

The Borchester Community Centre has three projects and operates from small premises. They employ a permanent centre coordinator and project staff are hired on a sessional basis. They have prepared the following information about costs.

◆ Centre coordinator's salary and national insurance **£16,000**
◆ Premises fixed costs amount to approximately **£15,000**
◆ Project A needs sessional staff costing **£3,000** and materials costing **£800**
◆ Project B needs sessional staff costing **£5,000**, additional telephone costs estimated at **£900** and extra print and stationery costs of **£1,000**
◆ Project C needs sessional staff costing **£4,000** and additional travel costs of **£500**

This information can be more usefully presented:

Project Costs	Project A	Project B	Project C	TOTAL
Sessional Staff	£3,000	£5,000	£4,000	£12,000
Materials	£800			£800
Additional Telephone		£900		£900
Extra Print and Stationery		£1,000		£1,000
Additional Travel			£500	£500
Total Direct Costs of Projects	**£3,800**	**£6,900**	**£4,500**	**£15,200**

Centre Fixed Costs	
Centre Coordinator's Salary and NI	£16,000
Premises Fixed Costs	£15,000
Contribution Needed from Projects	**£31,000**
TOTAL INCOME NEEDED	**£46,200**

The Borchester Community Centre needs total income of £46,200, but £31,000 of this relates to fixed costs and only £15,200 relates to projects. Each project needs to have sufficient income to cover its own direct costs and make a contribution towards the fixed costs of the organisation. Alternatively, a core grant is needed to cover the fixed costs.

This example draws out two points:

◆ you need to obtain funding that covers the direct costs of a project and also makes a contribution to the fixed costs of the organisation;

◆ the fixed costs will seem high in relation to projects unless you have enough projects. There will be a certain minimum of fixed costs (also known as core costs) for all organisations. You need to find the right balance between projects and core costs.

The contribution the individual projects make will be calculated by looking at the income of the project and deducting the direct costs.

Using Contribution Analysis for Decision-Making

The approach in the above example can be helpful, as it also highlights the cost saving if the organisation decides to close down one of the projects. None of the fixed costs would be reduced and the only saving would be the direct project costs.

In a similar way, it is unlikely that the fixed costs would change if the organisation started one more project. So the financial decision about taking on a new project hinges on the contribution the project will be able to make to the fixed costs of the organisation. In other words, does it bring in sufficient income to cover its direct costs plus some more? There would be a limit to the number of projects that could be run from the existing premises or coordinated by one member of staff, but until that limit is reached, maximum financial benefit is not being obtained from the money spent on overheads.

Once maximum capacity has been reached, the next project the organisation considers needs to be looked at carefully. In costing terms, the cost of taking on that project is not only the direct costs of the project itself, but also the whole of the increase in fixed costs that will be incurred because of the necessary increase in capacity. Because that project is forcing a move to new premises, additional core staffing, and so on, it must show that it can bring in enough income to make a sufficient contribution to these extra costs.

This may seem illogical in some ways. It could be argued that one project will not be able to carry a big increase in fixed costs and fixed costs should be spread fairly across all projects. The answer is that both views are correct. For the purposes of decision-making, you should look at the impact the new activity will have on the organisation. If the new project or activity will force up fixed costs, then those costs are associated with that decision. In financial terms, the new activity should only be taken on if it can cover all the costs associated with the decision.

Break-Even Analysis for Decision-Making

Break-even analysis is an extension of the process of identifying the contribution a project or activity makes. For the organisation as a whole to break even, the contribution from all activities must be equal to fixed costs. This is also true of smaller scale activities, such as fundraising events, where it can be useful to identify the fixed costs and the break-even point. Fundraising events can be high risk and this can be identified in financial terms by the probability of the event breaking even.

EXAMPLE

A Charitable Trust wishes to hold a charity concert for fundraising purposes. The event will be held at a concert hall which has a capacity of 5,000 people. There will also be a reception afterwards where wine will be served. The organisers plan to sell tickets at £10 and glasses of wine for £1. The concert hall will cost £1,000 to hire, publicity leaflets will cost £400 to print and wine will cost 50p per glass (sale or return basis). They will employ 10 waiters for the evening, who will be paid £50 each.

The fixed costs of this event are therefore:

Hall hire	£1,000
Publicity leaflets	£400
Waiters	£500
Total fixed costs	**£1,900**

With ticket prices at £10 each they only need to have 190 people buying tickets to break even. Every extra ticket they sell is pure profit. The organisers consider the likelihood of 190 people attending to be high, so the risk of this event is low. Any glasses of wine they sell will be profitable, as they make 50p on every glass sold. There is no risk attached to this. The financial risk they face is that they could incur the £1,900, but that the event is a complete financial failure (i.e. they make no money). So even though the risk that the event will not break even is low, they should consider whether they can afford to lose the amount of the fixed costs.

This is an example of using financial information to help in making a decision on whether to go ahead with an event or not. Often you are presented with choices – should we do this event or that event? Then the choice will be the event which shows the best return for the least risk. That is actually harder than it sounds, as return usually has to be reduced if you want to lower the risk.

Consider:
- What is the downside if the event goes wrong? What are the fixed costs that will have been incurred before we can stop? Are these non-returnable?
- What is the probability that it will break even? This is easier to judge if you can convert the break-even target into some tangible measure, such as number of people attending.

The figures used in the example above do not necessarily represent the full cost of that event. The costs of the fundraiser's time (if a paid employee) and the associated overheads would need to be taken into account if you wanted to fully cost the fundraising event. However, that is not useful for decision-making. You are already committed to the fixed costs of the fundraiser, and associated costs, so you have to live with those anyway. You need to look at the financial consequences of your decision to hold the event.

Overhead Apportionment

Having established the different types of costs of the organisation and gained an understanding of the cost structure, you can move on to the difficult area of overhead apportionment. The objective of apportionment is to assess the full cost of an activity so the basis of apportionment should be fair and reasonable. It should reflect the management time, administrative services, premises and other central costs that are utilised on that activity. The apportionment will have to be an estimate and is usually based on a measure such as:

◆ staff numbers
◆ staff costs
◆ number of clients
◆ amount of space used by department
◆ amount of income.

You may select different bases of apportionment for different overhead costs. For example, premises costs may be apportioned on the basis of space (square footage), whereas telephone costs may be apportioned on the basis of staff numbers. Since staff costs are usually a very high proportion of a charity's expenditure, this is most often used as the best indicator of the relative size of different activities, and therefore their relative use of central resources.

Understanding Apportionment

Apportionment is obviously estimated and can never be an accurate assessment of the true cost of an activity. There is little point, therefore, in spending too much time in detailed calculations and data gathering to carry out the apportionment exercise. It is also not worth arguing over the basis of the apportionment for too long. Everyone in the organisation should be told how the apportionment is undertaken, but should also be reminded that you will not be taking decisions to cut activities on the basis of the budgets which show the apportionments. As discussed above, decisions will have to be based on different financial data. The budgets showing apportioned overheads are for the purpose of calculating the full cost of an activity. This can be useful for fundraising purposes, and for identifying which activities generate surpluses and which require subsidy. All of the central overheads have to be funded and the most common method is by apportioning them to projects, thus including them in project fundraising applications.

Allocate Direct Costs

Overhead apportionment will be less contentious if there are fewer costs in overheads, and therefore a smaller amount being put down on each activity budget as overhead apportionment. It is better if you can identify more costs as direct and allocate these to the particular activity. For example, if a project is located in its own building, then it should be straightforward to budget and record the actual costs of the premises separately and allocate those costs directly to the project. You may decide to have a photocopier that requires a pass code before copies can be made, with a log being kept for the number of copies for each department or activity. This might work satisfactorily and should not involve too much extra work. However, trying to keep a log of copies by department by having a paper and pencil by the photocopier will probably be a waste of time. Somebody will have to spend time going through the piece of paper and calculating the use by department and trying to reconcile it to the register of copies on the photocopier. It is probably a waste of time to bother and an estimated apportionment will do just as well. You need to weigh up the value of the information against the effort required to gather it.

Funding Applications

As well as needing overhead apportionment for internal budgeting, you will need to consider how you will deal with apportionments when applying for funding. Some funders will reject any overhead apportionment, and some will automatically question an amount that seems to relate to central costs. The important thing to remember here is that a funding application is not the same thing as your own organisational budget. You should undertake the budgeting exercise for your own information and benefit, whereas funding applications should be prepared as a separate exercise, even though they will of course draw on the same information.

Presentation is the key, although you will, of course, have to heed any specific guidelines from the potential funder on what they will or will not fund. Here are three options commonly encountered.

1. The funder states that they will not fund any overheads apportioned to a project

You should therefore cost in all the incremental costs of that activity; the additional costs of the telephone calls, the installation and running costs of a separate telephone line, recruitment of staff and every pencil and paperclip! In this situation the new project may not provide a contribution towards the fixed costs of the organisation, but at least you should ensure that it is not a drain on resources. You may also wish to consider whether the new project will force extra hours of central administration, as it may be possible to cost this in your funding application.

2. The funder questions an amount shown in your funding application which relates to the overhead apportionment

One way to deal with this may be to explain what actual costs this relates to, by providing a brief outline of the organisation and how it is managed. For example, explaining the staffing and management, the premises, and how the organisation works. This is the rationale behind your budget and overhead apportionment method and needs to be explained. Try to pre-empt the question from potential funders by providing this explanation in notes to your funding application.

3. The funder has a policy of funding a fixed percentage for administration

You need to be clear on what it is that the funder will fund, obtaining clarification on what is included in the definition of administration and how the percentage should be calculated. Often it is a percentage of the direct costs of a project. This approach forces you to identify as many direct costs as possible and to prepare a more detailed budget than you might have done otherwise. You may be able to put some costs down as direct that you otherwise would have included in the overhead apportionment. For example, management of the project by the director or staff supervision may be allowed as a direct cost, even though it will in fact be an estimate and perhaps normally included in the overhead apportionment.

Cost Centres

The overhead apportionment will be undertaken to spread costs over different cost centres. These will be departments or areas of activity which are easily identifiable as logical ways to split up costs. Cost centre budgeting will work best when there is a natural way to identify the cost centre, such as following the management structure for the organisation. So if you have departments with managers in charge of those departments, it would be logical for them to have a cost centre budget to manage. Generally, the cost centres will be based on one of the following:

- geographical location (e.g. an area office)
- services provided (e.g. membership services, trading operations)
- internal departments or functions of the organisations (e.g. finance and administration, fundraising, education)
- funding received from particular sources.

For charities, it also makes sense to bear the Statement of Recommended Practice (SORP) in mind when considering the appropriate cost centres. The SORP requires charitable expenditure to be analysed by activity on the face of the Statement of Financial Activities. It also requires the cost of generating funds to be analysed into relevant catagories. This aspect of accounting is examined in more detail in Chapter 6. You may wish to check that you can easily convert your raw accounting information into final accounts that comply with the SORP.

Clearly, you will need to keep accounting records that will record actual transactions into the same cost centre structure. It is therefore wise to think about this aspect of the accounting process at the budgeting stage. You will need to be able to complete the bookkeeping for your cost centres without difficulty. For example, it should be possible to identify the direct costs of a cost centre quite easily. It is usual to set up the central administration of the organisation as another cost centre which will hold all the central management costs and other costs which are the overheads to be apportioned. You may want to split this into two cost centres (or more) if, for example, you decide to apportion premises costs on one basis and other costs on a different basis.

Example Cost Centre Expenditure Budget

Direct Costs	Information £	Advocacy £	Newsletter £	Helpline £	Outreach £	Central £	Total £
Salaries	45,380	23,577	32,654	56,027	25,920	52,035	235,593
Training	300	150	500	500	325	500	2,275
Travel	150	150	250	250	800	250	1,850
Recruitment	0	0	0	0	0	5,000	5,000
Volunteeers' Expenses	0	0	800	1,000	0	0	1,800
Publicity	0	0	500	500	600	1,000	2,600
Printing	500	250	5,000	0	0	2,000	7,750
Telephone	0	0	0	1,000	0	5,000	6,000
Postage	0	0	2,500	0	0	2,000	4,500
Stationery	0	0	0	0	0	2,500	2,500
Equipment	500	500	2,500	0	0	2,500	6,000
Accountancy/Audit	0	0	0	0	0	5,000	5,000
Premises	0	0	0	5,000	0	25,000	30,000
Total direct costs	**46,830**	**24,627**	**44,704**	**64,277**	**27,645**	**102,785**	**310,868**
Central Costs Apportioned							
Premises	8,750	5,000	6,250	0	5,000	(25,000)	
Other Overheads	19,446	10,112	14,001	23,336	10,890	(77,785)	
Total costs	**75,026**	**39,739**	**64,955**	**87,613**	**43,535**	**0**	**310,868**

Notes to the Example Cost Centre Expenditure Budget

Each area of activity has its own staff and some have volunteers. Additionally, there are some other costs which can be identified as relating to a particular project. The Helpline operates from its own premises, but uses many of the other resources available centrally, such as stationery and postage. Some projects have their own computers and other equipment, so the budget heading for equipment is directly allocated where possible and includes depreciation as well as any maintenance costs.

Central costs include the salary of the Director and support staff. All staff are recruited centrally, so the total costs of this are included in the central costs budget. Stationery is purchased centrally, although all projects use it.

Central costs are apportioned in two stages. Firstly the premises costs are apportioned to all but the Helpline on the basis of space occupied by each project. Secondly, all other overheads are apportioned on the basis of the staff costs of the project.

Calculations

For the premises apportionment, the space occupied was measured and the relevant percentage of the total calculated.

	Space occupied m^2	% space	Premises costs £	
Information	331	35%	8,750	
Advocacy	189	20%	5,000	
Newsletter	236	25%	6,250	
Outreach	189	20%	5,000	
	945	100%	25,000	

For the other overheads apportionment a similar calculation was undertaken, based on the staff costs of each project.

	Staff costs £	% staff	Other overheads £
Information	45,380	25%	19,446
Advocacy	23,577	13%	10,112
Newsletter	32,654	18%	14,001
Helpline	56,027	30%	23,336
Outreach	25,920	14%	10,890
	183,558	100%	77,785

Forecasting Income

The income budget is usually more sensitive than the expenditure budget and subject to fluctuations and change. You will need to make assumptions in order to make estimates of future income and these should be noted down and the most important ones provided with the budget. The estimates will not make sense to anyone without explanation of the basis. Different types of income will need slightly different techniques for forecasting, but it should be possible to group income into categories of:

◆ confirmed/definite
◆ probable
◆ possible
◆ uncertain/target.

Confirmed or Definite income will be when the source is known and the funds may have already been received. For example a grant or contract may have been awarded over a three year period, so the income for future years is certain. In budgeting it may also be useful to include income in the budget that has already been received, for example as restricted funds, but remains unspent. This makes sense when you are trying to match income and expenditure into the same budget period.

Probable income will describe sources such as committed and direct debit donations, subscriptions and some grants and donations where the funder has indicated that the funds will be forthcoming. Some calculation may be necessary to arrive at a sensible forecast figure for the budget. For example, one has to assume that only a certain percentage of regular income from subscriptions or direct debit giving will be received, because people may cancel or move banks. Past experience may help you to arrive at the percentage, which may be quite high (say 95% of the amount of current subscribers), but you should also take into account activities to increase membership or regular giving.

You may also be using fundraising techniques such as raffles, direct mail, or applications to companies and charitable trusts. If your charity has experience of the method of fundraising, then it may well be reasonable to include an estimate of such income under the category of probable. If your charity has no experience, then it is wiser to decrease the amount expected and push the income source down into a lower category of 'possible' or 'hoped for'.

Possible income may include new sources of funds, or new funds from existing sources. So it may be that the charity is trying a new form of fundraising and it will have to estimate the amount it may receive. It usually takes some time to establish a new fundraising method, so the estimate in early budgets should be low. New fundraising methods can be included in this category, where the plans have been made and it is definite that the fundraising effort will take place. This category can also include the income from new members or new covenants where there is some planned activity to recruit new members or new donors.

Uncertain/Target income will be appropriate for the as yet unknown sources of income, where it is clear that the charity will need to find further funds. This may also include new or untried fundraising methods or fundraising for which there is no detailed plan. Obviously, one should not have too much income in this category!

Income budgets should be rooted in the fundraising plan, which should give full details of the costs and forecast income for each method of fundraising. The fundraising plan has to be achievable and should include reasonable estimates of forecast income. The targets set for fundraisers may not be suitable as the source for the income budget. It is more prudent to include a lower estimate of forecast income in the budget, to ensure that there is not a deficit.

The timing of fundraising will be crucial to the financial stability of the organisation, and this is examined more closely in the section on cashflow forecasting (see below). Some charities adopt a policy whereby they raise the funds first and then start the spending plan. This may not be possible for charities which are fundraising to fund current spending, but it is worth considering as a policy for the uncertain income in the fundraising plan.

Cashflow Forecast

The revenue budget concentrates on the forecast income compared to expenditure, matching particular costs to the related source of funding. The budget will usually look at the overall figures for the year, arriving at a surplus or deficit for the year. So the revenue budget may show that the organisation can break-even over the year. In practice, however, the timing of cash inflows and cash outflows will not necessarily coincide. The cash position may actually be very bad at some points during the year, even though the position may improve by the year end. A cashflow forecast will help you to manage this aspect.

The cashflow forecast should be based on information in the budgets, but it should also forecast when actual receipts and payments will occur. In effect, you are predicting what your bank statements will look like. Usually cashflow forecasts are prepared on a month by month basis for the forthcoming year, however, in times of crisis, you may plan cashflow weekly. In a period of expansion and change you may wish to extend the forecast period to eighteen months, two years or even three years.

The cashflow forecast will include information from both the revenue and the capital budget. It is concerned only with the actual cash flowing in and out of the organisation, not which budget heading it comes under. It will exclude depreciation, as this is a notional cost, not a cash payment. It will include the full price paid for new fixed assets acquired. It will include loans advanced or repaid, as well as receipts and payments regardless of which financial year end they relate to.

Updating the Cashflow Forecast

The forecast is more useful if it is regularly updated. You may wish to change the forecast amounts to actual amounts when these become known, or insert an extra column alongside each month for actual receipts and payments. More importantly, you should review the future forecast figures and check that the amounts and the timing still seem valid. Better information may have been received and cashflow forecasts need constant updating.

Interpreting the Cashflow Forecast

Your attention should be drawn to the bottom line of the cashflow forecast. This tells you the forecast balance at the bank at the end of each month. If this is a negative figure, then you are going to be overdrawn. If it is a positive figure, then this is the estimate of cash balances available. Either way, you may need to take action. A general rule is to try to make the timing of cash outflows coincide with the timing of cash inflows.

If there are months when the cashflow forecast shows that you would go overdrawn, then you may be able to look through the receipts and payments in more detail and see which of these can be brought forward or delayed. It is worth remembering that there is little point in delaying payment of a bill for £500 when the overdraft is going to be £5,000. You may lose the goodwill of a supplier and you will not necessarily avoid the overdraft by tinkering with several small amounts. It is better to look at the bigger items and the structural problems. Is the problem that you always estimate that income will come in earlier than it actually does?

Using the Cashflow Forecast – Practical Steps

1. Consider the various sources of income and put in appropriate descriptions as headings on the left-hand side.
2. Group expenditure into fewer categories than usually found in a budget – 'office overheads' for example, rather than rent, rates, heat, stationery. As long as no one item would severely distort the overall picture, then this would be sufficient detail.
3. Enter the amounts expected to be received or paid in the appropriate month on the appropriate line.
4. Total the receipts for each month (A).
5. Total the payments for each month (B).
6. Calculate the receipts minus payments for each month and enter the result in the monthly cashflow line. A negative result indicates higher payments out for the month than receipts (A) - (B) = (C).
7. Brought Forward means the balance in the bank at the beginning of the month (D). For the first month, this should be the figure from an agreed bank reconciliation (i.e. bank statement balance adjusted for outstanding items). You can draw up a cashflow forecast at any time during the year, not necessarily just for financial years.

Example - Cashflow Forecast

Months	1	2	3	4	5	6	7	8	9	10	11	12	TOTAL
Receipts													
Fees													
Donations													
Grants													
Investment Income													
Loan Advance Received													
Total Receipts	A												
Payments													
Net Salaries													
Inland Revenue													
Project Costs													
Office Costs													
Capital Purchases													
Loan Repayments													
Total Payments	B												
Net Cashflow for Month	A-B=C												
Balance Brought Forward	D	E											
Balance Carried Forward	C+D=E												

8. Starting with the first month, you should calculate the total of the monthly cashflow figure and the balance brought forward. This will give you the balance to carry forward to go into the box on the line Carried Forward (C) + (D) = (E).

9. The balance to carry forward at the end of the first month is the balance brought forward in the next month, and so on.

Cashflow Considerations

You need to know and understand the financial operation of your organisation well in order to plan the cashflow. Consider the following questions and timing of activities to come up with a list of factors which will affect cashflow.

- What are the historic patterns for receiving fundraising income?
- How is earned income spread over the year?
- When do we receive grants, bank interest, investment income and so on? Do we receive this income in advance or in arrears?
- Have we been realistic in forecasts of income from new projects?
- Have we made an allowance for bad debts on earned income?
- Have we included tax reclaims for covenants and gift aid in accordance with the expected timing of the claim and receipt?
- Have we made allowances for staff changes and the time lag involved when recruiting new staff?
- For new projects or developments, is there a lead-in time whilst the project is being set up with initial costs built in to the cashflow?
- Are payments for capital projects or new equipment included in the month when the expenditure is expected?
- Does interest receivable or interest payable reasonably reflect the balance at bank through the year?

VAT in Cashflow Forecasts

If the organisation is not registered for VAT, then all payments should be shown inclusive of VAT and income will not be affected. This is the same basis as for the budgets. If the organisation is registered for VAT, then receipts and payments should include VAT, but you will also need to prepare a VAT calculation or estimate the amount of VAT which will have to be paid over or recovered from H M Customs and Excise each quarter. VAT can have significant effect on cashflow and so should not be completely ignored.

Chapter 2

FINANCIAL REPORTING AND MONITORING

Once budgets and forecasts have been agreed, it is essential to monitor them. For this reason, financial reports are a key management tool, both for the senior paid staff and the trustees. You will need to think about how different reports will be needed by different people in the organisation. For example, the trustees do not need the same level of detail as a departmental manager. You will also need to consider the reporting timetable quite carefully, to ensure that information provided is recent enough to be useful.

BUDGET COMPARISON

The mainstay of management accounts is a comparison between the financial plan and the actual amounts recorded in the books. So the revenue budget should be compared to actual income and expenditure, for example. It is important that the comparison is a valid one, in other words that you are comparing like with like. Check that you are following a few simple rules.

1. The headings should be the same in the budget as in the accounting records. (It is no good trying to compare a budget for stationery to actual expenditure for printing, postage and stationery).
2. The time period should be the same (obviously six months budget should not be compared to seven months actual).
3. The basis of the figures should be the same (it is no good comparing total cash paid out on an insurance premium for a year to a budget figure of six months insurance costs).

Flexing Budgets

You sometimes need to make adjustments to the basic budget figures in order to make valid comparisons. Seasonal variations or a development plan may mean that income and/or expenditure does not occur evenly through the year. It may be inappropriate to take a full year's budget and simply divide everything by two to create a budget for the first six months. Look at the situation of an expanding staff team, for example. You may have allowed for two extra staff for the second half of the year. Whilst this may be the equivalent of one staff member all year for the purpose of calculating the budget, a misleading impression could be given by comparing actual expenditure for the first six months to a simple half of the budget figure. So you should calculate the expected expenditure for the first six months and then compare actual expenditure for the first six months to those figures.

It is also possible to flex budgets in a slightly different way. Supposing you had prepared a budget on the basis of a plan which forecast that a new project would come on line in month 4. The project implementation is delayed by three months. You can therefore flex the budget to take the project out – re-forecast, in effect. Then compare budget to actual and you must explain any further variations from the plan. By flexing the budget, you have really removed one cause for differences.

If your income and expenditure has a seasonal pattern, then it may be wise to prepare budgets on a quarterly or even monthly basis. You then have a budget which is already flexed for the seasonal differences.

When working with committees, it can cause problems if the budget seems to be a 'moving target'. In this case, it may not be appropriate to present a flexed budget, but it is still a good idea to undertake the calculation as part of a variance analysis (see below).

Variance Analysis

The difference between the budget and actual amounts of income and expenditure is known as a variance. Significant variances need to be investigated and their cause identified. You should be able to analyse a variance by comparing the details of actual performance to the details of the original financial plan. The notes on assumptions underlying budget estimates will now be useful to help you analyse the financial information. Variances will most often be caused by one or several of the following:

◆ a change in price
◆ a change in volume
◆ a change in timing.

It is important to recognise the cause so that appropriate action can be taken. Is the variance reflecting a permanent increase in price which means that the budget should be revised? Does a drop in volume (e.g. number of members) mean that income targets were far too optimistic and should be adjusted? Or is it just a delay and all will be well by the end of the year? Asking the right questions and carrying out the right sort of variance analysis will help groups to take corrective action if necessary.

Example - Variance Analysis

The budget showed membership income to be £11,690, whereas actual income is £10,300, an adverse variance of £1,390. To analyse the cause of the variance, we need to compare the variables separately:

(F) = Favourable
(A) = Adverse

(S) *MEMBERSHIP SUBSCRIPTION RATES*

	Budgeted Rates £	Actual Rates £	Variance £
Individuals	18	20	2 (F)
Family	27	25	2 (A)
Junior	8	5	3 (A)

	Budgeted Numbers	Actual Rates £	Fixed Budget £	Original Budget £	Variance £
Individuals	350	20	7,000	6,300	700 (F)
Family	170	25	4,250	4,590	340 (A)
Junior	100	5	500	800	300 (A)
				Total Variance	**60 (F)**

(N) *NUMBERS OF MEMBERS*

	Budgeted Numbers	Actual Numbers	Variance Numbers	Actual Rates £	Variance £
Individuals	350	290	60 (A)	20	1,200 (A)
Family	170	150	20 (A)	25	500 (A)
Junior	100	150	50 (A)	5	250 (F)
				Total Variance	**1,450 (A)**

OVERALL VARIANCE	£
(S) due to rate change	60 (F)
(N) due to volume change	1,450 (A)
Total Variance (N - S)	**1,390 (A)**

Much simpler variance analysis will be the norm, so it should be easy to provide explanations for variances in management reports. It is also useful to identify whether the variance is because of a permanent change, such as a price change, or whether the variance is caused by a timing difference. A timing difference might be caused by a delay in implementing a plan or because certain functions always happen at a certain time of year and your budget does not deal with seasonal differences. An example of a simple explanation of a variance would be as follows.

The budget forecast that 10 staff would be employed and that their salaries would be increased by 4% for inflation. Actually, one person left halfway through the year and the post was left vacant. The salary increase was actually 3.5%. Working this out in financial terms tests the validity of the explanation and demonstrates that you can explain the whole of the variance. So this example translates into numbers as:

Savings due to vacant post	£7,728
Savings due to lower increase	£513
Total variance	**£8,241**

Monitoring Key Factors

The whole management accounting process becomes much easier when you gain a full understanding of the key factors in your organisation which affect financial management. Far too much time is wasted monitoring minor details which will make no big difference to the organisation even if they do show a large variance. It is much better to think about the main drivers and focus attention on these. They may be obvious, but you will need to think about the consequences of things going wrong to pick them up.

Some examples are given below.

◆ An organisation running training courses needs a certain number of people on each course in order to break even. So they need a system which monitors the number of people registering on courses on a very regular basis, even daily. This may not even come from the financial accounting system, as this sort of information is likely to be on a database.
◆ A key factor for a housing charity will be the number of empty properties or beds, as they will only receive funding or fees for occupied spaces. Usually the empty spaces are valued at the rate that would have been received for them.
◆ Some projects will be operating on a fixed expenditure budget, so for them the amount they are spending will be important. It may be more useful to know how much has been spent and how much has been committed by way of orders or decisions. The total then tells them how much of the budget allowance has been taken up and how much is left.

The format of management accounts should reflect the type of organisation and give due emphasis to the key factors. This will probably mean that a lot less detail is included in management reports on fixed costs and overheads and other costs which do not vary a great deal, such as salaries. On the other hand, more attention may need to be given to cashflow items, and monitoring cash balances, debtors and creditors.

Monitoring Cashflow

Even charities which have healthy cash balances should monitor their cashflow and liquidity. The focus of their attention might be to improve their treasury management, whereas a charity with limited resources may be focusing their cashflow monitoring on the ability to pay the creditors on time. The difference in emphasis may well affect the method adopted for monitoring cashflow, but in fact the principles are the same.

The end of year balance sheet is a helpful starting point for assessing liquidity and it is essential that management accounts include a balance sheet. This indicates at the very least that the accounts do balance and gives some degree of reassurance on the accuracy and completeness of the accounts, provided there is proper reconciliation of key balances in the balance sheet, such as the bank balances (see Chapter 5).

The balance sheet items under current assets and current liabilities will be of most interest in monitoring the cashflow and liquidity. These are the items which make up the working capital of the organisation. Its working capital needs can be assessed by measuring the likely levels of the components under the balance sheet headings.

Current Assets

◆ Stock
◆ Debtors
◆ Loans to others
◆ Prepaid expenses
◆ Short term investments
◆ Bank accounts
◆ Petty cash floats

Current Liabilities

◆ Loans from others
◆ Bank overdrafts
◆ Amounts received in advance
◆ Trade creditors
◆ Accrued expenses
◆ Tax and National Insurance
◆ VAT

For the purposes of management accounts, some of these headings will be less important than others. It will not usually be necessary to have very accurate figures for prepaid and accrued expenses unless these are very significant. Similarly, the amounts received in advance do not have an impact on liquidity, as these will not have to be paid out, even though they are technically creditors. However, the cashflow forecast should show the expenditure on the projects the money has been received for. Stock will be a key factor to be monitored if you are running a business, but not if it is a very minor part of your activities. Charities which carry a small stock of publications should not put a lot of time and effort into counting stock for management accounts.

From the balance sheet, you can then work forwards to a cashflow forecast which predicts the cash inflows and outflows. My preference is for a cashflow forecast which combines all the bank accounts of the organisation, effectively treating them as one. Some people prefer to only show the current account on the cashflow forecast. Either way, the cashflow forecast should show the surplus funds or deficit at the end of each month. This should be reasonably accurate for a few months ahead. Appropriate action can then be taken to invest or try to reschedule receipts/payments. As a last resort, loans or bank overdrafts may have to be sought. Remember that this is the most expensive form of finance available. However, it may be necessary whilst fundraising plans are put into place and take effect.

Managing in a Crisis

The cashflow forecast in this context is a management tool and a live document, needing regular updating to reflect changing circumstances. It is important that you date each version, so that you know which one is the most recent. This is the management tool most needed by finance managers and chief executives in organisations experiencing cashflow difficulties. It will help with day to day decisions such as:

◆ Which creditors should we pay today, this week, next week?
◆ Can we afford a new piece of equipment?
◆ Should we advertise this post or delay recruitment for new posts?
◆ Can we delay items of expenditure? Will this have any impact on income?

Cashflow is the key aspect of finances, allowing you to monitor your organisation and to be aware as early as possible of potential financial difficulty. The examples below are typical mistakes.

◆ Continuing to spend in accordance with an agreed budget, but ignoring the cashflow implications.
◆ Using the brought forward reserves to fund expenditure – fine as a theoretical way of balancing a deficit budget, but a significant problem if the reserves do not exist in cash.
◆ Spending on capital projects without monitoring this or planning adequately for the cashflow impact; this can happen easily in organisations where there is undue emphasis on monitoring revenue budgets.

- Spending on fundraising where the type of fundraising requires a large initial cash outlay. This is not the best type of fundraising when a charity is short of funds.
- Committing funds to fundraising with a long payback period.

Managing Cash Flow in a Crisis – Action Points

- Exercise good credit control – chase debtors for prompt payment.
- Review charging policies – can you ask for cash in advance instead of in arrears e.g. book orders, subscriptions, services?
- Bank receipts daily.
- Ask major suppliers for special payment terms and then stick to them.
- Investigate payment of certain overheads by instalments, e.g. insurance, equipment maintenance.
- Pay small bills promptly and avoid wasted time dealing with them.
- Prioritise major payments.
- Defer action that will lead to additional expenditure, such as recruitment, taking on leases, purchasing equipment.

If the organisation is in a cashflow crisis, it will need to consider three important points.

1. Can the organisation deal with the short term consequences? Action on credit control, stock control, or deferring expenditure may deal with the short term problems.
2. Can the organisation come up with a long term plan to tackle the underlying problems? The reasons for the cashflow crisis may be complex and relate to changed funding, underfunding of projects or core activities, an imbalance between the costs of administration and the amount of activity, historic overspending, excessive fixed costs, or failed initiatives, just to give a few examples.
3. In the light of the answers to the above two questions, the organisation must consider whether it can continue its activities. If it is a limited company, then the directors are bound by company law to cease trading when they can no longer pay their debts. This means that the directors should not continue to commit expenditure when they do not know how they are going to pay for it. This includes paying out net salaries when the funds to pay the tax and National Insurance are not available. Trustees of unincorporated charities also need to exercise care, because they will be personally liable to pay the debts of the charity if it becomes insolvent. This will include redundancy pay to staff where it applies.

Using Ratios

More and more charities are effectively running businesses, albeit charitable businesses. One therefore needs to consider any business methods that might be useful in monitoring the activities of the charity, including ratios and performance indicators. Ratios are more useful as a measure because they indicate the level of something or the rate at which something is done. In financial management, ratios can be used to indicate the level of money owed to an organisation and measure how quickly debt is collected. Here are a few suggestions for ratios that might be useful in setting targets and monitoring performance.

Aged Debtor Analysis

If you sell goods or services on credit, then you will probably operate a sales ledger. If this is on a computerised accounts package, then it may have the facility to produce a list of 'aged debtors'. This will analyse your debtors showing month by month how much they owe according to the month in which they were invoiced. You therefore see very easily from the totals how long the debts have been outstanding. Commonly the headings are current, one month old, two months old, three months old and over three months.

Whilst the aged debtor analysis is useful for prompting action to collect debts, the calculation of a ratio will help you to see whether you are getting better or worse at debt collection. You can calculate the average number of days it takes the organisation to collect a debt, or 'days debtors', and then check this on a regular basis.

$$\frac{\text{Total debtors}}{\text{Sales per day}} = \text{Days Debtors}$$

There are several ways to calculate the sales per day. It does not matter which way you perform the calculation, as long as you are consistent. A fairly conventional way to calculate it is:

$$\text{Sales per day} = \frac{\text{turnover for year}}{365 \text{ days}}$$

For example, at the end of the month you may have £8,000 of debtors relating to unpaid invoices for services, the total income from which is £48,000 per year. So sales per day are £48,000 divided by 365 days = £131.51. The days debtors is calculated by dividing £8,000 by £131.51 = 61 days. So debtors are taking an average of 61 days to pay. Your invoice terms are 30 days, so debtors are taking a month longer to pay on average. This inevitably means that some people are taking even longer, so you need to think about credit control strategies. The effectiveness of those strategies can then be monitored by checking the days debtors monthly. Note that ratios are useful because they are describing the rate or proportion of something. The days debtors ratio tells us the proportion of sales which are uncontrolled debts. Even if sales increase, the proportion is still a constant measure.

Rent Arrears

A variation on the debtors ratio is a ratio which measures the amount of rent outstanding compared to the total rent receivable. This is usually expressed as a percentage or the number of weeks rent the arrears represents on average. For example, rent arrears of £34,000 compared to total rent receivable for the year of £320,000 gives a percentage of 10.6%. Convert this into weeks by calculating the average rent receivable for one week (£320,000 divided by 52 weeks = £6,154) and then dividing the rent arrears figure by the weekly rent roll (£34,000 divided by £6,154 = 5.5 weeks). This means that on average, tenants are five and a half weeks overdue with their rent. Targets can then be set and the arrears levels monitored through the ratio.

Occupancy Rate – Housing and Residential Care Charities

Charities providing housing or residential care will need to monitor occupancy on a regular basis and usually do so by measuring the empty spaces or voids. The voids rate is the percentage of voids compared to the total income potentially receivable. To make a valid comparison you need to value the voids at the rate of income which would have been receivable had the space been occupied.

For example, a hostel for young homeless people has spaces for 20 people each night and each space is normally eligible for funding of £10 per night. So total possible income for one week is 20 x 7 x £10 = £1,400. The register shows that they had 3 empty spaces each night. The value of voids is therefore 3 x 7 x £10 =£ 210. The rate of voids is £210 divided by £1,400 = 15%. The organisation can set itself a target in the budget to lower the level of voids to 10%, and than monitor actual against this.

Return on Fundraising

Business measures will be applicable to a great many fundraising efforts. An overall measure for comparing different fundraising methods and different activities looks at the return the fundraising produces compared to the direct costs involved. For example, one might be able to measure the return on a raffle by counting up the cost of the prizes, printing the tickets, sending out the tickets and any other direct costs (say this amounts to £3,000), then looking at the cash received for the sale of raffle tickets (say £15,000). The rate of return in relation to expenditure is therefore:

$$\frac{£15,000}{£3,000} \times 100 = 500\%$$

The expected rate of return for a particular type of fundraising will also help in setting budgets, as well as monitoring performance.

Gross Profit Percentage

Gross profit percentage is a key ratio for many types of trade, such as retail selling of bought-in goods (not donated goods), mail order selling, Christmas card sales and other forms of merchandising. Calculate the gross profit percentage as follows:

$$\frac{\text{Gross profit}}{\text{Sales}} \times 100$$

Different rates of gross profit can be expected for different types of goods, but monitoring the percentage both overall and for individual lines will provide useful management information about performance.

Sales per Square Foot

In retailing, it is usual to measure the gross sales income compared to the amount of space occupied. This may be useful for comparing the performance of shops in different locations, as well as comparing performance from one week/month/year to the next. Simply calculate by dividing sales by the number of square feet occupied.

Presenting Your Information

Graphs and Pictures

Graphs and pictures can be a very useful way of presenting financial information, however care must be taken to use them appropriately. Graphs will only focus attention on one particular aspect at a time – pie charts that are cut into more than about four pieces become very difficult to read.

Graphs and pictures are best used in conjunction with some well written text – they break up the text and highlight important aspects. Do not use graphs to excess or present graphs on some trivial matter, or your point will be lost. You also need to consider the right sort of graph for the type of information you are presenting. In general, people choose between pie charts, bar charts and line graphs for financial information.

Example Pie Chart

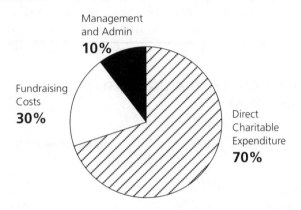

Management and Admin
10%

Fundraising Costs
30%

Direct Charitable Expenditure
70%

Example Bar Chart

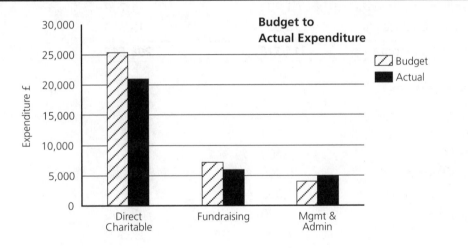

Budget to Actual Expenditure

Legend: Budget, Actual

Example Line Chart

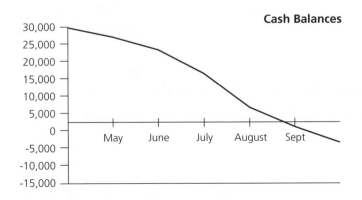

Cash Balances

Case Study – Simple Management Accounts

The following management accounts have been prepared for presentation to the management committee. Look at the report and compile a list of good and bad points about it.

BORSETSHIRE ADVISORY TRUST ANTICIPATED OUTTURN
FINANCIAL YEAR 2002/03

	Original Budget £	Likely Outcome £
INCOME		
Grants and Fees	244,818	244,818
Shop sales	36,000	20,000
Donations	10,000	10,000
Fundraising	5,000	4,000
Bank Deposit Interest	1,700	1,700
Trading Co Receipts	18,000	18,000
(A) Total Income	*315,518*	*298,518*
EXPENDITURE		
Salaries	220,362	205,593
Training	2,332	2,332
Travel	1,200	1,200
Recruitment	6,500	2,600
Volunteers' Expenses	1,800	1,600
Publicity	2,500	2,500
Printing	7,500	7,500
Telephone	6,000	6,000
Postage	4,500	4,000
Stationery	3,500	2,500
Equipment	6,400	6,400
Accountancy/Audit	8,000	9,725
Premises	28,885	30,000
(B) Total Expenditure	*299,479*	*281,950*
SURPLUS/DEFICIT (A-B)	**+16,039**	**+16,568**

BORSETSHIRE ADVISORY TRUST FINANCIAL YEAR 2002/03
BUDGET TO ACTUAL FOR NINE MONTHS TO 31 DECEMBER 2002

KEY:
◆ *The variance shown is the difference between nine months budget and nine months actual*
◆ *Figures in brackets under the variance column mean that income is less or expenditure more (bad news).*
◆ *Figures not in brackets mean that income is better or expenditure less (good news).*

	Budget For Year £	Budget for 9 Mths £	Actual for 9 Mths £	Variance £	Notes to Accounts
INCOME					
Grants and Fees	244,818	183,614	174,058	(9,556)	1
Shop sales	36,000	27,000	14,966	(12,034)	2
Donations	10,000	7,500	9,930	2,430	3
Fundraising	5,000	3,750	3,713	(37)	
Bank Deposit Interest	1,700	1,275	1,333	58	
Trading Co Receipts	18,000	13,500	6,878	(6,622)	4
Total Income	***315,518***	***236,639***	***210,878***	***(25,761)***	
EXPENDITURE					
Salaries	220,362	165,272	150,474	14,798	5
Training	2,332	1,749	2,332	(583)	
Travel	1,200	900	663	237	
Recruitment	6,500	4,875	1,301	3,574	6
Volunteers' expenses	1,800	1,350	803	547	
Publicity	2,500	1,875	1,213	662	
Printing	7,500	5,625	3,695	1,930	7
Telephone	6,000	4,500	4,624	(124)	
Postage	4,500	3,375	921	2,454	8
Stationery	3,500	2,625	1,526	1,099	9
Equipment	6,400	4,800	3,667	1,133	10
Accountancy/Audit	8,000	6,000	1,725	4,275	11
Premises	28,885	21,664	6,674	14,990	12
Total Expenditure	***299,479***	***224,610***	***179,618***	***44,992***	
SURPLUS/DEFICIT	**+16,039**	**+12,029**	**+31,260**	**+19,231**	

**BORSETSHIRE ADVISORY TRUST FINANCIAL YEAR 2002/03
FINANCIAL MANAGEMENT REPORT UP TO 31 DECEMBER 2002**

Budget to Actual For Nine Months – Notes to the Accounts

The budget figures are the budget for the year 1997/98 as approved at the management committee on 13 February 1997. These have then been apportioned to nine months by simply taking three-quarters. The Actual for Nine Months figures are the accruals basis income and expenditure figures prepared from the accounting records for the first nine months of the financial year.

Significant Variances

The variance column shows the difference between the budget for nine months and the actual for nine months. The notes below explain the significant variances.

1. The grants income is less than expected because the council have not yet actioned the increased level of grant funding agreed verbally with them. We assume this will be paid in the final quarter, which is still outstanding.

2. Shop sales are much lower than expected. This seems to be due to over-optimistic budgeting and the long sickness of the shop coordinator, causing the shop to be open for fewer hours.

3. Donations are higher than expected for the nine months, due to a legacy from one of the users who died last year. However, no further amounts are expected.

4. Trading company receipts are lower than expected because the transfers from the trading company have been delayed. A separate report to the trading sub-committee shows that net income should reach the budget for the year. A significant transfer will be made from the trading company before the end of March.

5. Salaries are lower than expected for two reasons: a) the pay increase had not been implemented on time and this will have to be backdated. This will be put through payroll at the end of January and amounts to £3,456 including National Insurance contributions; b) the post of advocacy coordinator has been vacant for three months and the post of administrative assistant has been vacant on and off for six months. The recruitment for a new advocacy coordinator has been undertaken and a new person will be in post at the beginning of February. The administrative assistant recruited earlier left because she found a better paid job and a new round of recruitment has commenced.

6. Recruitment costs are lower than expected as the personnel manager has changed the advertising policy and expensive adverts in national newspapers are no longer required. This will affect the budget for the year and projected expenditure on this item can be significantly reduced.

7. Printing costs are lower than expected, but this was due to a delay in the reprinting of a large number of forms and stationery items. This will now happen in the last quarter of the financial year.

8. Postage is low compared to budget because the petty cash expenditure was not analysed for these accounts, although a quick review suggests that this will be lower than budget anyway. This is probably because the budget was too high.

9. Stationery is underspent because the budget was too high. It is likely that printing and stationery budgets overlap and some costs have been budgeted twice.

10. Equipment includes maintenance and depreciation. The underspend may well be used up by the end of the year.

11. Accountancy/Audit budget includes the amount for the year end work, which will have to be accrued in the year end accounts, but the accrual is not in these management accounts. The actual expenditure relates to advice during the year, which was not budgeted.

12. Premises costs are under budget, because the correct amount of rent has not been charged by the council. We will have to accrue the full amount in the budget when we do the year end accounts, even if we do not know the actual rent to be charged.

Case Study Analysis

Good Points

- The report states when it was prepared and by whom.
- There is a key to explain the variances.
- The Budget to Actual report for nine months shows the budget for the year as well.
- The likely outturn, in other words what the final figures are likely to be, is given as well.
- There are notes to explain significant variances.

Bad Points

- There is no information on cash balances, debtors, or creditors, because no balance sheet is provided.
- Also due to the lack of a balance sheet, there is no information on the reserves (funds) levels of the organisation.
- It seems likely that no balance sheet has been prepared, which undermines the confidence we may have in these figures. This is indicated by the comment on postage; if the petty cash expenditure has not been analysed, then where is the total spent through petty cash shown? Maybe the expenditure shown is incomplete in other ways.
- Some accruals have been missed off, such as premises. The bad effect of this is counteracted by the provision of the likely outturn figures.
- It would be better to show the likely outturn figures on the same page as the comparison between actual and budget.
- There is no departmental or activity based analysis of income and expenditure, so we do not know which areas are doing well or badly. In particular, shop and fundraising expenses are presumably included under other headings (such as printing, postage, stationery, premises), but they ought to have been identified as separate departments, so that we can see

the contribution made by fundraising activities to the organisation. (Contribution is direct income less direct expenses; see Chapter 4 for further explanation and examples.)

◆ There is no analysis to show restricted funds and the related expenditure. Monitoring restricted funds and their use is an important aspect of monitoring financial management.

Summary

Key points of good financial management

◆ RECENT – Each month's committee meeting should be presented with figures up to the end of the previous month. Out of date management accounts have no value as management information.

◆ RELEVANT – Attention must be focused on the key figures, and this is partly achieved by reducing the level of detail so that questions like 'why are bank charges £10 over budget?' do not get asked. The right information needs to be available to different people.

◆ RELIABLE – The completeness and accuracy of the accounting records should be ensured by monthly reconciliations. In addition, the preparation of a balance sheet as well as an income and expenditure account ensures that the management accounts have been correctly drawn from the accounting records. Reliability does not mean 100% accuracy, since estimates have to be made in some areas of accounts and speed will sometimes have to take priority over accuracy.

Chapter 3

FINANCIAL CONTROLS AND MANAGING RISK

It is important in any undertaking that proper control is exercised over the resources available. It is even more important for charities because they handle public money and receive special tax benefits. Since trustees are responsible for ensuring that the charity uses all funds received for its charitable purposes, they should take a special interest in the establishment of proper financial systems and controls.

RISK

Like any other entity, charities are at risk of loss of funds or assets, or that funds will be misapplied. It may be helpful to consider the controls appropriate in most charities in the context of the risks that exist.

Broadly, there are two types of risk:

♦ internal risk of fraud or mismanagement, which can be minimised by good controls and procedures;
♦ external risk of outside events affecting the organisation in a detrimental way. These are events outside the control of the organisation and management can only plan to mitigate the effects of such events.

Internal Risk

The risk that something will go wrong internally is higher in organisations where the control environment is weak. This will possibly be marked by some or all of the following:

♦ lack of formal or written procedures
♦ authority to commit the organisation rests with inappropriate people, usually individuals who are too junior, or too inexperienced
♦ lack of reporting to the trustees, so paid staff are making key decisions
♦ staff are not properly trained
♦ trustees do not understand their responsibilities towards the beneficiaries

- ◆ the wrong culture exists, for example a senior staff member treats the charity as if it were their own company, claims large travel and subsistence expenses, and acts without the authority of the trustees
- ◆ poor staff morale or personnel problems
- ◆ a dispute between trustees, or between staff and trustees, for example on the future course the organisation should take.

A poor control environment as described above may well lead to fraud, or financial malpractice. However, good financial controls are not just about preventing fraud; a lack of controls can also lead to expensive mistakes and unauthorised expenditure. A poor control environment should concern both staff and trustees. Many cases have shown that when things go wrong, allegations of fraud and malpractice are frequently made. Every staff member and trustee should be able to rely on good controls, in the knowledge that this is a form of protection for them as well.

Monitoring Financial Plans

One of the important ways in which trustees can exercise control over the affairs of a charity is through the planning cycle (see Chapter 1). It is essential that trustees approve the organisational budget in advance of its implementation. Once the budget has been approved, this is a mandate to staff to implement the plan. This will involve committing the organisation to costs, so it is important for staff that they have the authority to do so.

The trustees can exercise significant control by monitoring the organisation's performance against budgets. Trustees should receive regular reports to show them an overview of the financial state of the organisation and comparisons of actual performance to budgets. Trustees should also ask for explanations of significant variances and recommendations for action (see Chapter 2).

Financial Procedures

The other key aspect of internal financial control is to have adequate procedural checks. The trustees are responsible for ensuring that proper procedures exist and that they are implemented. One way for them to fulfil their duties is to require that a financial procedures manual is prepared. Whilst it will take time and effort to draw up a manual, it is a task which can be undertaken gradually. Copies of memoranda and example forms can be accumulated and the notes built up section by section. A manual will need regular updating and there is no point in insisting on difficult or time-consuming procedures which no-one follows. It should be a practical guide for staff and trustees, useful for the induction of new members, and a source of reference for all. Auditors will also be able to make use of it, and their time will be saved as they will not need to write so many systems notes. They should review the manual and comment or make any recommendations for changes. It will not be adequate to adopt the financial procedures of another organisation. No two organisations operate in quite the same way and the objective is to operate procedures that work.

The financial procedures manual can be more comprehensive if you wish and incorporate policy statements on various areas, such as reserves levels. The example given below is an outline manual, not comprehensive, which could be summarised into a few pages if you prefer.

Example – Financial Management Procedures Manual Contents

1.	**Introduction**	How to use this manual.
2.	**Organisation chart**	Who is responsible for what with respect to finances?
3.	**Budget setting**	Timetable and responsibility for setting budgets; suggested format and headings; method of allocating overheads.
4.	**Reports**	Frequency and type of report; examples of format; notes on how reports are prepared.
5.	**Banks**	Details of bank accounts held and cheque signatories; purpose or use of bank accounts if any are specific.
6.	**Income**	Details of procedures for opening post, banking receipts, invoicing, handling cash and so on; example forms.
7.	**Expenditure**	Authorisation limits for approving expenditure; procedures for large, unusual or one-off expenditure; system for approving and paying invoices.
8.	**Payroll**	Procedures for documenting and communicating new staff appointments, staff leaving and changes in pay rates; method of payment for staff and authorisation of payment.
9.	**Petty cash**	Levels and types of expenditure which may go through petty cash; who may authorise petty cash expenditure; how system should be reimbursed and record-keeping.
10.	**Staff expenses**	How expenses will be reimbursed, what type and level of expenditure; who may authorise staff expenses.

Internal Controls

Procedures will only be effective if they incorporate adequate internal controls. These may be arithmetic checks or checks that something that has been paid for does exist. The various internal controls should ensure that the accounting records are complete and accurate, and that the assets of the organisation are properly looked after. The different types of internal controls possible are:

- physical
- arithmetical and accounting
- authorisation and approval

- segregation of duties
- supervision and training
- organisation and management.

Physical Controls

These are concerned mainly with the safeguarding of assets. Procedures should be designed so that access to assets is only permitted to authorised personnel. In other words, you need to keep equipment, cheque books and petty cash in safe places, preferably under lock and key. You also need to consider proper insurance cover in the event of fire or theft.

Arithmetical and Accounting

Bookkeeping systems incorporate certain checks and balances, such as control accounts, trial balances and reconciliations. They also include systems such as sequential numbering of invoices so that their completeness can be confirmed. There should be checks that invoices and accounting records are correctly totalled and analysed.

Authorisation and Approval

All transactions should require authorisation or approval by an appropriate responsible person. Limits for authorisation should be set, so that really minor items do not have to wait for the trustees' approval, but conversely that major expenditure does not happen without their approval. The approval should always be documented, for example by a signature on a petty cash voucher or a minute of the trustees' meeting.

Segregation of Duties

This is a way of organising the responsibilities for various aspects of the whole chain of events in such a way that different people provide a check on each other. It is not simply to prevent fraud, but to provide a check to detect errors. Poor segregation of duties will allow one person to instigate, authorise and record a whole series of events which commits the organisation to significant expenditure. Good segregation of duties will separate out different aspects of the transaction such as ordering, approval and payment, and ensure that different people have different roles at each stage.

Good segregation of duties can be difficult for small organisations, but they still need to consider this. It is quite reasonable to ask trustees to take a more active role if the charity has few staff. At its very simplest, the internal control system should separate the task of approval or authorisation of expenditure from the recording of payments.

Supervision and Training

Any system of internal control will depend on the quality of the supervision and training of staff or volunteers. It will be up to the treasurer and senior staff to identify training needs and provide supervision and support to staff undertaking finance tasks.

Organisation and Management

The structure of an organisation – with reporting lines, budget holders, budgets and management accounts – should focus on the responsibilities of each post, not individuals, and should ensure that the right work gets done at the right level.

Implementing Good Internal Controls

Some areas of internal control deserve special mention, as they can cause particular problems in charities.

Post Opening Controls

In charities where a significant amount of unsolicited donations are received through the post – often in cash – it is essential that the post opening procedures are strong. Unopened post should be kept securely, and when it is opened, two people should be present and a list made of all cash/cheques received. Someone different should bank the cash/cheques, preferably the same day. It will then be possible to check that all monies received were banked. It is possible that collusion between two staff could take place to misappropriate incoming cheques, but this is not common. An additional measure would be to rotate staff, which would be appropriate where high levels of cash and cheques are received in the post.

Cash Collections

Collecting tins or boxes should be sealed and prenumbered, with a log to keep a record of the numbered tins sent to collectors. Two people should be present when the tins are opened, and the cash banked as soon as possible.

Fixed Assets

Trustees must safeguard the assets of the charity and ensure that they are used for the charitable objects. Equipment can be a difficult area to control, especially as trustees are not involved in the day to day running of the charity and therefore not physically present themselves to ensure that assets are kept secure and properly used. It is essential therefore that there is a fixed assets register. This is an inventory or list of all the major items of equipment, showing when purchased, the cost, location and condition. Further details can be added, to make the list as useful as possible. If there is a theft of property, it will be useful to have a record of serial numbers of equipment or other details for the insurers. You may find it useful to keep a note of the replacement cost for the purposes of assessing the insurance cover needed. Depreciation can be calculated and recorded on the fixed asset register. Having established a register, it is essential that periodic checks are made; someone needs to physically check the existence and condition of the equipment and compare that to the information on the register.

Cheque Payments

The signing of cheques is an important control in charities; the cheque signatory is authorising the withdrawal of funds from the bank for the purpose stated. It is usual for charities to require two signatures on every cheque, but this may be an ineffective control in reality. The value of the control exercised by the second signatory will be lost if the individual just signs everything without actually checking it, or if they sign blank cheques in advance. It may be better therefore to consider carefully who the cheque signatories should be, allowing one person to sign on their own up to a certain value. For small charities, the trustees will have to be involved in signing cheques to a greater degree, as any other procedure compromises segregation of duties. It is better if the cheque signing can be organised properly into weekly or fortnightly batches, so that cheque signatories have a proper chance to look at the supporting invoices or other documentation before they sign. It is bad practice to ask signatories to sign a cheque as they are rushing out the door, or to sign incomplete cheques, for example where the payee details are not completed. Such situations can generally be avoided by planning ahead.

Make sure that cheques are made out properly to the full name of the payee; abbreviations can lead to fraud if the cheque gets stolen on its way to the recipient. For example, B. T. can easily be changed to B. Thompson. Make cheques for your telephone bill out to British Telecommunications Plc.

Cheques do get lost and stolen in the post and therefore it is worth looking at other ways of paying people that avoid the postal system. The Banks Automated Clearing System (BACS) is available from all high street banks and transfers money direct from your bank account to the bank accounts of recipients. You have to set up the account details of people you regularly pay, such as staff and suppliers, but can then execute a whole batch of transactions with one set of signatures. As well as being more secure, it also saves time on writing out lots of cheques. You need to contact your own bank about setting up this payment system.

Staff Costs

For many charities, staff costs may be up to 80% of total expenditure. Good controls here are essential.

Controls should start at recruitment and selection. A job description and person specification should have been approved at the appropriate management level. Clear procedures should be set out for the selection process and these should be made known to all persons involved in recruitment. References should always be sought, in writing and with a telephone call. This would identify a bogus reference, and is more likely to produce useful information where the previous employer has been reluctant to commit themselves on paper to the shortcomings of the potential employee. You may need to take up three references for certain staff involved in cash handling, as this is often a requirement of fidelity insurance policies.

Once an employee is in post, regular performance appraisals will help the organisation deal with problems and hopefully remove some of the causes of fraud. Fraud is often perpetrated by disgruntled employees or those with problems outside work. These situations can be prevented by good staff supervision.

If the staff team is small and everyone works set hours, then the monthly salary cost will be very stable, with a low risk of fraud or error. In larger organisations, or where staff are paid on hours worked, there need to be controls to ensure that payments are made for work actually done and at the proper rate. For example, in residential care charities, there is usually a staff rota which is planned in advance. Actual hours paid should broadly agree to the rota and variances should be explained. Obvious targets for fraudulent activity are false overtime claims, false timesheets, and fictitious employees. The checking and authorisation of overtime claims and timesheets has to be taken seriously. Training may be needed for those responsible for this area.

Implementing Good Internal Controls

This example is for a small organisation, where segregation of duties is more difficult. There is only the director and administrator at the central office and all other staff are project staff.

1. Project leader prepares order for new equipment, confirming at the same time that this is within the budget for the project.

2. Director approves order and initials copy as evidence of approval.

3. Order sent by administrator.

4. Goods received at project. Project leader signs despatch note and passes it to administrator as evidence that goods received in good condition.

5. Administrator receives invoice from supplier and checks to despatch note and copy purchase order, and checks arithmetical accuracy of invoice, initialling invoice and coding to correct project and budget heading.

6. Administrator prepares cheque and cheque payment form, and presents with invoice to cheque signatories.

7. Cheque signatories sign cheque, thus authorising the disbursement of funds from the organisation's bank account. They also initial the cheque payment form.

8. Administrator enters cheque payment in the cash book, analysing according to budget heading and project code.

9. Administrator prepares a bank reconciliation at the month end.

10. Treasurer reviews the bank reconciliations and checks that they have been properly prepared once a quarter.

Cash Transactions

Cash transactions are always more vulnerable to fraud and error, so they should be avoided where at all possible. Since cash cannot be completely avoided, then much stricter controls have to apply. Petty cash should be kept on a float (imprest) system, whereby it is topped up to a fixed amount. The amount drawn from the bank will not be a regular amount, but will represent the actual amount spent out of petty cash since the last top up. Do not use petty cash for inappropriate things. It should only be used for buying small sundry items, such as milk and supplies, cleaning materials, possibly stamps and small stationery items. Petty cash should only be topped up from the bank; keep any incoming cash separate and bank it intact.

Avoid paying salaries in cash. You may have to use cash to pay the cleaner and to reimburse volunteer's expenses, but ensure that the proper paperwork is maintained. The payment to the cleaner is still wages and should be considered part of the payroll. Volunteers should still be completing expenses claim forms, even though they are paid through petty cash.

Expenses Claim Forms

Staff and volunteer expenses is an area where charities need to exercise great care. There should be a proper forms system for claiming expenses and it is better to have separate forms for staff and volunteers. Expenses should be claimed regularly, say monthly. An appropriate person has to authorise the expenses as reasonable and necessary. The head of a department or a project leader should authorise the expenses for staff in their teams; the chief executive would probably authorise the expenses of the heads of department; the chair or treasurer will have to authorise the chief executive's expenses; the volunteer coordinator will probably authorise the expenses of volunteers; and the chair and treasurer will have to authorise the expenses of other trustees and each other.

Receipts should be attached to the expenses claims and adequate explanation given for the reason the expense was incurred. It is wise to have a written policy on the type of expenses which may be claimed and what it is that may be charged. Clear guidance at the outset may prevent problems later.

Expense Floats

Staff may be given expense floats, but the float should be a reasonable amount. The float can only be topped up when evidence of expenditure is provided, which can be entered on the normal expenses claim. The float should be documented and staff should sign a form acknowledging receipt of the float. If they leave, they will have to repay the float, so there must be a clause in their contract of employment giving you the power to deduct such a sum from their net salary. The float should not, therefore, be too large. The staff float system can work in place of a petty cash system for small charities or small projects. It has the advantage that one person is accountable for it and that a petty cash tin, so often the target for thieves, is not on the premises.

Credit Cards

Staff can use their own credit cards for purchases and they should claim reimbursement through the normal expense claim process. A company credit card scheme may be appropriate for charities where staff and trustees have to travel a great deal. Care must be taken, however, that proper expenses claims are still received from all individuals using the card. The temptation is to ignore the paperwork when the bill gets paid anyway.

Internal Risks Relating to Law and Regulations

Charities are subject to charity law, of course, but many other laws apply equally to charities as to any other entity. Care must be taken that the charity's procedures incorporate checks and controls to ensure that the charity complies with the law as it applies to that particular charity and its area of operation. Breach of the law will frequently cost the charity a great deal in penalties or damages. Examples of areas where problems frequently arise are given below.

◆ PAYE legislation requires an employer to deduct tax and National Insurance and pay it to the Inland Revenue for all employees. Not applying the PAYE procedures to casual employees and sessionals/consultants when the Inland Revenue consider that these people should have been on the payroll will result in significant liabilities. Similarly, paying volunteers in a way that jeopardises their volunteer status will cause PAYE problems.

◆ Health and Safety regulations apply to a large number of charities and you must ensure that you have complied with the regulations. A good source of reference is *The Health & Safety Handbook* (Directory of Social Change, 2001).

◆ Employment law is changing quickly and charities are frequently taken to Employment Tribunals. The costs of mistakes in this area are high, so it will be cheaper to get proper advice on employment at the outset.

◆ Restricted funds must be spent in accordance with the donor's stated wishes. Charities must ensure that their procedures identify incoming restricted funds and then apply proper checks that the funds are spent appropriately. Trustees may be personally liable for a breach of trust.

◆ VAT registration is compulsory if the organisation goes over the registration threshold, with penalties for late registration. Penalties are also due if large mistakes are made and found on an inspection visit. Charities need to ensure that they take appropriate advice on VAT issues.

◆ Charities may find themselves inadvertently trading, especially when undertaking new types of fundraising (see Chapter 9). This could lead to tax liabilities and censure by the Charity Commission. Proper advice is needed before embarking on new ventures.

Internal Audit

Internal audit is one way for trustees to ensure that proper procedures are in place. Internal auditors will look for improvements in efficiency and economy, looking into all the operations of the charity, not just the finance function. Only large organisations can afford to employ full-time internal auditors, but some charities do operate a shared arrangement and others use volunteers to undertake certain tasks that are part of an internal audit programme.

In considering areas for internal audit, you need to look at the risk profile of the different aspects of the charity's operations. Areas where there is a high risk of fraud, or other financial loss to the charity, will be targeted first and subject to more rigorous checks. The risk profile will be an assessment of the likelihood of various events taking place, together with the consequences to the charity if they do. This should not be restricted to purely financial events. For example, petty cash tins are vulnerable to theft, and this may cost the charity a few hundred pounds over a year. However, a serious incident which harms a child in the care of an employee of the charity might irreparably damage the charity's reputation and consequently its ability to raise funds. Which is the more important risk to guard against?

Audit Committee

The internal audit team should have a clear line of reporting to an independent body of people, usually the audit committee. The audit committee should be made up of a few trustees and other non-executive people, possibly co-opted for their technical expertise in this area. An internal audit will not be sufficiently independent if it only reports to the finance director or chief executive. It should ultimately report to the audit committee, which will also be responsible for agreeing the priorities for internal audit attention and the programme of work for each cycle. Clearly, senior management do need to be involved in the internal audit process, but they should not be allowed to control it or block it.

Risk of Insolvency

A major concern for trustees is the risk of insolvency, especially where they are held personally liable for any outstanding debts.

Limited Liability

Only companies and Industrial and Provident Societies give members limited liability. This means that the individual trustees/directors are protected financially if the organisation goes bankrupt, although they can still be held liable if they were negligent in any way, for example by allowing the charity's assets to be used for purposes outside the charitable objects.

The trustees of a trust, charity or unincorporated association will be personally liable for the debts of the organisation if the charity has insufficient funds to pay them. This could be a significant amount if the charity has paid staff who are entitled to redundancy, or if there are other contractual obligations such as a premises lease. Once a charity has significant contractual obligations it would be appropriate for it to consider incorporation, and therefore the benefits of limited liability. If a charity knows that it intends to employ staff or take on premises, then it is wise to choose an incorporated structure from the outset. Incorporation means that the organisation is a separate legal entity and only the assets of the charity, not individual trustees or directors, are at risk if the charity goes bankrupt.

Incorporating a Charity

Many charities begin as an unincorporated association or trust and decide later that they wish to enjoy the benefits of limited liability. It is not possible to convert an existing charity as such; the process involves the setting up of a new charity and the transfer of all assets and liabilities to the new charity. This also means a new charity number, new bank accounts, and inevitably new stationery, so it can be an expensive and time-consuming process. It can be more convenient from a financial perspective to time the changeover to coincide with the end of the financial year. The new charitable company must have been set up and registered with the Charity Commission in advance.

Since the new company must have its first financial year end more than six months but less than eighteen months after incorporation, it should be possible to keep the same year end after the changeover. You will need to submit final accounts for the old charity to the Charity Commission, showing a nil balance sheet after the transfer of assets and liabilities to the new company.

It is not possible to incorporate a charity with net liabilities. The trustees of the new charity would not be allowed to accept the liabilities, as to settle these from new monies may not be applying the funds to the charitable objects. Additionally, the creditors of the old charity are protected in this instance and the trustees of the old charity do not escape liability by incorporating.

Incorporation may help trustees to sleep at night, but it does not mean that one can then ignore the risk of insolvency. Good practice in financial management means that you exercise budgetary control and monitor the financial position of the organisation on a regular basis. Insolvency rarely happens overnight and the organisation should be able to see the warning signs early. The trustees then have to weigh the benefits of the various options available to them and act in the interests of the beneficiaries.

External Risks

External risks are the events which the organisation has no control over, some examples of which include:

- ◆ loss of funding
- ◆ fire, flood, landslide, or any other natural disaster
- ◆ legal actions

- changes in political environment
- changes in legislation
- market forces.

In responding to these threats, you have to consider strategies to mitigate your losses, because you cannot stop the event itself. The response will obviously vary, depending on the nature of the threat.

Diversifying Income

Many charities are dependent on one major source of funding in their early years; as the charities mature, they usually try to spread the range of their funding sources. This is a way of spreading risk, so that the loss of one particular source of funding does not then mean closure of the charity.

Managing Fixed Costs

Organisations which will be significantly affected by external changes in the political and legislative environment should consider maintaining their flexibility by keeping down their fixed costs. For example, campaigning groups need to be able to respond quickly to new events. This will be easier if they can gear up to larger scale activity for a short while, and then scale down again. Maintaining a large infrastructure all the time will be costly and may lose them support. High fixed costs will also be a problem for organisations dependent on few sources of funding. If you have built up the central administration of an organisation to cope with projects which only have three year funding, you must have a strategy for dealing with the wind-down to a smaller infrastructure after that funding ceases.

Scenario Planning

Having contingency plans for future events that may threaten the organisation can prepare you to handle an external risk. Working through some 'what if...?' questions and thinking through the consequences may also affect your plans and help you to ensure that the threat does not affect you too much.

Insurance

Some external risks can be covered by insurance. Employer's liability insurance is compulsory for organisations with paid staff (and advisable for those with volunteers only), and organisations should have insurance against the risk of fire, theft and flooding. In fact, there may be other areas to consider for insurance, for example, if your organisation gives advice, you may want to cover it in the event of a legal action being brought against you for negligent advice. Organisations should always check the terms of the cover carefully and review all insurance annually. Cover needs to be adequate and cover the risks the organisation has.

Time Period of Commitments

It is unwise to commit the organisation to long term expenditure when the risks are that long term funding will not be there. Lease commitments for equipment and premises may tie the organisation into committed expenditure for time periods which go beyond the funding horizon. When organisations are young and the external threats to its existence very real, then it would be better to minimise these types of commitments.

Reserves Policies

The objective of having unrestricted funds in reserve is to enable the charity to cope with unplanned events. Very often, the effects of the event can be managed in the long term, but the charity needs reserves in the meantime. There is no rule on how large reserves should be; this will depend a great deal on the nature of the charity's activities and the level of external risk perceived by the trustees. It will also depend on what other action the charity is taking to mitigate the effects of the external threats, as this will affect the level of reserves required. For example, a charity with high fixed costs will need high levels of reserves in order to cope with the effect of a reduction in income. Another charity might take action to reduce the level of fixed costs and will not then need such high levels of reserves.

Separate Company

A separate company, which may be charitable or not, depending on its objects, could be set up to undertake some of the activities of the organisation, particularly trading. This is a way of mitigating the effect of the failure of one area of activities on the rest of the organisation. Some charities have set up separate companies to undertake contract work to ensure that charitable reserves are not used to support the contract activity in the event of problems. This might be a useful strategy to deal with certain types of external risk, but it is not a substitute for proper assessment of the risk of the new venture. If the venture is too risky to undertake in the main part of the charity, then one has to consider whether it is too risky to undertake at all.

Summary

Many of the controls necessary for the proper management of a charity often seem to create extra administrative work and costs, so some charities try to skimp in these areas. Whilst it is quite right to try and keep administrative costs to a minimum, this should not be done at the expense of good financial controls. Internal controls and regular review of external risks will help to ensure the safety of the charity's funds and its ability to fulfil its objects.

A checklist of Common Control Weaknesses and How to Avoid Them

◆ *The payee details on cheques may be the initials of the charity.* If the cheque falls into the wrong hands, the payee could be amended to an individual's name. For example, a cheque made out to B.T.C. could be altered to B.T. Collier. It is therefore wise to have a rubber stamp with the full charity name on it, which can be used to complete the payee details properly.

◆ *Purchase invoices could be presented twice for payment, without the cheque signatory necessarily noticing.* This can be a deliberate technique for defrauding an organisation, as the second cheque to the supplier is diverted into another bank account. Purchase invoices should be cancelled with a rubber stamp PAID or in a similar way.

◆ *Copies of purchase invoices are presented for payment.* Copy invoices could be duplicates or they could be invoices to another organisation with the details changed, which can be done relatively easily on photocopies. Payment should never be made on copy invoices, only original ones.

◆ *Payment is made to a supplier on the basis of a statement, without the original invoices.* This may lead to payments being duplicated and should therefore be avoided.

◆ *A dummy supplier could be set up, or a friend could be set up to send in dummy invoices.* The check on despatch notes should help to eliminate some of these, if segregation of duties is operated properly. Special care may be needed when it is a question of services, where no despatch note is received. The person approving the invoice for payment should be considering whether the services have actually been received.

◆ *A relative of a member of staff or a trustee undertakes the building improvements for the organisation or provides computer consultancy or other services.* Whilst they should be providing services on fair terms, this might be in doubt if the contract was not won on a competitive basis – how will the organisation know that it is getting value for money? Contract services need to be properly ordered and a tender procedure followed where the amount involved is significant. This usually means that at least three potential contractors are asked to tender. This will apply to building work, but also consultancy work and services of all sorts. If a tender is not appropriate, then the terms and conditions should be set out in a letter of appointment, setting out what the expectations of the contractor are.

◆ *Cash is drawn from the bank to purchase items of equipment from retail stores, because the retailers will not accept a company cheque.* It is usually possible to arrange for cheque payment on the day of purchase, or to purchase the goods on a pro-forma invoice. The supplier will release the goods once the cheque has cleared. Another option is to give a staff member a float (making a cheque to them personally, rather than cash) and make them accountable for the use of the funds. They have to provide a breakdown of all expenditure on a claim form and provide all receipts. This may be appropriate when the charity is moving to new offices or opening a new project.

CHAPTER 4

INVESTMENT

DUTIES OF TRUSTEES

Charity trustees have a duty of care to the beneficiaries of their charity in all the areas of their responsibility, but this is particularly brought into focus when it comes to investing the charity's assets. The Trustee Act 2000 sets out the trustees' duty to maximise the value of the assets and therefore to invest them to obtain a good return. However, they should not risk losing the assets by investing in highly speculative, high risk ventures. They must balance risk against return.

Trustees must also balance the future needs of the charity against the current needs, so they should consider whether the maximisation of income for current use is in the best interest of future beneficiaries, i.e. will it mean a loss of capital growth and hence income growth? Trustees need to balance long term capital growth against short term income generation.

Capital growth should be, at the very least, sufficient for assets to maintain their value compared to inflation. In practice, most investment advisers are trying to beat inflation and obtain much better capital growth as well as producing some income. It will depend on whether the priority is for income generation or capital growth as to how the balance between these two factors is struck.

A total return approach to investing aims to maximise the overall investment return, rather than specifying the amount expected in the form of income and the amount in the form of capital gain. The capital gains, divdends and interest are pooled.

Charities with a permanent endowment historically have had to allocate capital returns to the permanent endowment fund and income returns were available for distribution. In May 2001, the Charity Commission issued new operational guidance which allows permanently endowed charities to apply for permission to operate a total returns approach to investment. The charity may then allocate some of the capital gains to distributable income.

Trustees' Considerations

When investing the charity's assets, the trustees should consider:

◆ whether the charity's investments are sufficiently diversified. This means that the charity should not put all its eggs into one basket and risk losing a large part of its assets on a single investment;

◆ whether the investments are suitable for the charity. This refers to the need for a charity to consider what are suitable investments for the size of the charity, the amount to be invested and the time period over which it wishes to invest;

◆ whether a particular investment vehicle is suitable as one of its kind. This means that trustees should consider whether the particular investment is too risky, is speculative or is in any other way inappropriate.

Ethical Investment

Particular attention has been drawn to the duties of the trustees in respect of ethical investment through various court cases. One of the better known cases was brought by the Bishop of Oxford against the Church Commissioners in 1991. His case was that the Church Commissioners should not be investing in certain types of companies, including those which were active in the defence industry and in South Africa (this was at a time when apartheid was still being actively pursued as a policy in South Africa). The argument was that such investments were contrary to the Christian ethic. The Bishop did not win the case, because the judge ruled that the trustees' first consideration must be to maximise the return on investments. Ethical considerations can be taken into account by trustees, but it should be because they are in the interests of the beneficiaries, not because of the trustees' personal values.

It may be appropriate for certain charities to avoid certain activities when considering their investment criteria, because such investment would be in conflict with their charitable objects. For example, a cancer charity may wish to avoid investment in the tobacco industry. This is justifiable, because clearly the promotion of smoking is contrary to the charity's objects and not in the interests of the charity's beneficiaries.

Since the ruling in the above mentioned case, more funds have been set up to reflect the public interest in ethical investment and charities may wish to look at these as possible investment vehicles. However, trustees should take care to examine the return on their investment carefully. There should be no problem if the ethical fund produces a return that is expected to be at least as good as the return on another fund.

Powers to Invest

The Trustee Act 2000 came into force on 1 February 2001 and applies to all charities set up as trusts or unincorporated charities, but not to charitable companies. The Act sets out a new general power of investment, which allows a trustee to place funds in any kind of investment, excluding land, as though he or she is the owner of those funds. There is also now a separate power to aquire land as an investment.

If the governing document restricts powers of investment, then this restriction or exclusion will still apply. The investment powers for charitable companies will be set out in the Memorandum and Articles of Association.

For charities now covered by the Trustee Act 2000, this new general power of investment is wider than that previously allowed (under the Trustee Investments Act 1961). You will need to ensure that the existing portfolio is appropriate, given these wider powers.

Investment Policy

Every charity should draw up an investment policy, even if they have only small sums to invest. Even placing funds on deposit at the bank is a form of investment. There is an overlap here with the reserves policy of the charity, which will need to be clear first. The trustees are not directly achieving the charitable objects by investment of the funds; they will be producing income or increasing the capital of the charity, which may then be applied to the charitable objects.

The investment policy should look at several points, including the following:

◆ Does the charity need to generate income from the investment, or is the priority to maximise capital growth?
◆ Does the charity need access to the funds at short notice? Can some funds be identified as available for long term investment?
◆ What risk is the charity prepared to accept and what is permitted under the charity's investment powers? How should the charity diversify its investment portfolio in order to minimise the overall risk to the charity?
◆ Are there any ethical considerations which the charity can legitimately pay heed to?
◆ For long term investment, is there a preference for a managed portfolio of investments, unit trusts or common investment funds?

A charity with an endowment fund may find it relatively easy to work out its investment policy, whereas a charity which only has surplus working capital may need to undertake its financial planning first. The outline cashflow forecast for at least the next two years will be needed in order to draw up the investment policy. Having been drawn up, an investment policy must be kept under review. The trustees should review it at least once a year, but also if there is a significant change in circumstances or a sudden new influx of funds, such as a substantial legacy.

TYPES OF INVESTMENT

Trustees have to make choices about the type of investment they think is appropriate. Most charities will look to stocks and shares (either directly, or indirectly, through pooled funds) for their investment choices, although where permitted they may also consider property. The risk profile, time horizon and likely returns will determine whether the type of investment is suitable for a charity at all. Trustees will also need to consider their investment objectives to assess whether the type of investment is suitable for the position of their particular charity. Generally, the options available to charities are as described below.

A Deposit Account with a bank or building society. These accounts usually offer immediate access, or they may be on 7 day, or other notice periods. The rates of interest will usually increase as the amount invested and the notice period increases. Charities should still consider the risk of placing large sums with one bank or building society. Although one can consider really big high street banks to be almost risk free, this cannot be said for some of the smaller financial institutions. Recent banking collapses should serve as a warning that things can go wrong and depositors can lose their money. One should be wary about interest rates that seem to be very high compared to other banks; if the return seems too good to be true, then it probably is! As a precaution, charities should establish whether the bank is a member of a deposit protection scheme. Regulations came into force on 1 July 1995 ensuring that compensation of 90% of the sum deposited up to a maximum of £20,000 would be paid to depositors in the event of a default by a bank or building society, which is a member of such a deposit protection scheme.

A Common Deposit Fund is a special deposit fund available only to charities in England and Wales. The fund is itself a charity and it is a system of pooling cash deposits from many charities so that the amount available for investment is increased and the return improved. The fund manager will invest the pooled fund with several different banks or deposit takers, so the risk is spread. They are often investing overnight or for a day at a time, offering easy access to funds. Interest is paid gross, so the whole sum is immediately available without the necessity for tax repayment claims. Some managers even provide a cheque book with this type of account.

Equities are the shares of companies. Companies pay out dividends on their shares, usually twice a year, although there can be no guarantee as to how much the dividend will be. The market value of the shares can go up or down, but mostly one is looking for capital growth as well as dividend income. The risk of investing in equities can be reduced by spreading the investments across a portfolio of shares in different companies. The risk can also be reduced by choosing blue chip companies – the top UK companies with a good track record of paying out dividends and capital growth. Investing in foreign companies quoted on overseas stock exchanges is usually perceived as being higher risk.

Gilts are fixed interest securities such as government stocks. These include loan stocks, bonds, debentures and preference shares issued by central and local government and companies. They are known as gilt-edged securities, hence gilts, because the rate of return is fixed and the risk of loss of capital is low. The rate of return is low compared to equities, and capital growth is unlikely. Most balanced portfolios include some gilts as a way of balancing the risk profile of the other elements. National Savings Bonds are a form of gilt and are often used by charities with small amounts to invest where they cannot afford to risk their investment. The return should compare to a deposit account, but there may be a penalty if you sell before the maturity date, thus making these unsuitable if you need to access the funds at short notice.

A Unit Trust is a pooled investment fund which invests in quoted shares. These will be wider range investments and often specialise in a certain area or you may choose a general trust. The past performance of different unit trust funds can be examined to help in the choice, but this will not necessarily guarantee future performance. This is a form of investing in a portfolio of gilts and equities which is more diversified than could be achieved by a charity with a relatively small amount to invest. However, there are charges or commissions made by the fund manager and care should be taken that you find out what these are when you are comparing different unit trusts. Many unit trusts charge entry and exit fees in addition to annual management fees. There is also no guarantee on either the income or the capital of these funds.

Common Investment Funds are pooled funds, similar in many ways to unit trusts, but with additional benefits for charities. Common Investment Funds (CIFs) are approved by the Charity Commission and registered as charities. An independent board of trustees determines the fund's investment policy and the trustees have the same responsibility as any charity trustee to maximise returns within the constraints of reasonable risk. The advantage of CIFs is that they are spreading risk, because the pooled funds are invested in a range of different stocks and shares. These are tax-free and therefore carry the advantage of paying out income gross. In addition, the administration charges are much lower than for ordinary unit trusts. Note that these are not available to charities in Scotland and Northern Ireland.

Property will only be a suitable investment for charities with large funds available for investment and the power within their governing instrument to do so. It will also only be suitable as a small proportion of the total portfolio. Property is a long term investment and cannot usually be sold quickly should the charity need access to the funds. Specialist advice will be needed to help trustees assess the prospects for capital growth and risks associated with returns. Trustees may also need to consider that there will be costs involved in managing and maintaining the property. It is not appropriate for trustees to speculate in land deals or to enter into development deals, as the returns for the cash investment are highly variable.

Derivatives are generally contracts for a deal at a future date which are bought and sold in the hope that a profit can be made. They include futures, options, interest rate swaps and foreign currency deposits. These are highly speculative and the risk of loss is high, whilst the probability of a high return is quite low. They are not suitable for charities and are best left to the traders in the market. Charities may wish to buy foreign currency if they know they have a future commitment and wish to fix the exchange rate of that transaction. This is a legitimate use of derivatives and is not speculative, rather, it is hedging the risk of foreign exchange rate movements in the period before the currency is needed.

Works of Art are not usually used by charities as an investment vehicle, nor do governing instruments generally permit it, as there is no income or certainty of capital growth, and an investor has to be able to wait until the market conditions are right for a sale. This is different to charities buying such items in fulfilment of their charitable objects, in which case the purchase would not be classified as an investment.

Size of Investment

Before embarking on an investment strategy, trustees need to decide whether they have enough to invest. Because of transaction costs, and entry and exit costs for certain investment vehicles such as unit trusts, it is uneconomic to buy and sell shares over short periods of time. You therefore need to be fairly sure that the funds you invest can be left intact for a reasonable period and will not be needed at short notice.

You will also need to have a reasonable sum of money to make the exercise worthwhile. It will not be worthwhile setting up a portfolio with a fund manager unless you have at least £500,000 – £1 million. The Charity Commission advises CIFs for charities with funds of less than £1 million.

Working Capital

Trustees need to leave sufficient working capital available at fairly short notice for the immediate needs of the trust and some contingencies. Careful monitoring of the cashflow should inform the trustees over a period of time how much is likely to be needed in working capital. You would have to take into account planned changes and fundraising activities. It may be useful to think about the working capital needed in terms of a number of months of running costs. For example, a charity running services and paying salaries will need to think about how long it is committed to those costs. From this exercise, the trustees may decide that they need to keep at least three months salaries and running costs immediately available, with a further three months working capital available at three months' notice. The balance of funds could be invested over a longer term, thus maintaining some flexibility within the portfolio for access to some funds at short notice.

Treasury Management

The trustees can still exercise good treasury management over the funds held for working capital. This also applies to trusts which do not have large funds and therefore do not plan to invest in the longer term. This involves cashflow forecasting and monitoring of the funds necessary for day to day finances. Only funds immediately needed should be held on current account, with additional funds held on deposit. Banks offer a range of options for the best management of day to day funds and this should be discussed with the charity's bank manager. Common deposit funds will also be available. You do need to keep the situation under review, as interest rates change and the types of deposit accounts available vary.

Investing in Stocks and Shares

If the trustees decide that they do have sufficient funds to invest in stocks and shares, then they need to consider how this is to be managed.

◆ *Direct Management* of a portfolio of stocks and shares. Trustees who are suitably qualified could directly buy and sell their own stocks and shares. This still has to be undertaken through a stockbroker, although a share shop could be used. Transaction costs are kept down, but trustees may be vulnerable if there was a fall in the value of the portfolio, since they would not be able to show that they had taken appropriate advice.

◆ *Advisory Management* means that the trustees obtain advice on the selection of investments, but retain the decision on the actual buying and selling of investments themselves. The financial adviser can be an appropriately qualified trustee or employee, although this can cause some problems if the portfolio falls in value. Consequently, many charities consider it more appropriate to obtain independent advice in investment matters. If a firm of fund managers is used, then it will usually buy and sell as nominee holder of the shares and deal with all administration. This is a significant advantage as the administration can be onerous if equity shares are held over a period of time, due to matters such as scrip issues, rights issues, take-overs and mergers.

◆ *A Discretionary* portfolio is where an investment manager would manage investments on behalf of the trustees. The charity will have to pay the investment manager's fees for this service and the portfolio would have to be balanced to ensure that risk is spread. In order to get the necessary diversification, this option is only suitable for charities with very large funds to invest (probably at least £1 million).

◆ *A Common Investment Fund* would be more suitable for those with smaller amounts to invest. Advice should be sought on a suitable fund, although trustees might be able to interpret the comparative data on the performance of various CIFs published regularly in *Charity Finance*. The funds are approved by the Charity Commission and currently monitored by them, and because they operate like unit trusts, the risk is spread over a portfolio of investments held by the fund. Additional advantages are that the income is received gross, CIFs have independent trustees and they are cost effective.

Appointing an Investment Manager

Under the Trustee Act 2000, trustees have the power to employ agents to manage the charity's assets. There should be a written agreement with such agents and their performance should be kept under review.

Custodian Trustees

There can be practical problems for unincorporated charities in holding shares, and more particularly transferring shares. This arises because the charity is not a legal entity itself and cannot therefore own property; the trustees must hold the shares on behalf of the charity. This problem can be avoided by the use of custodian trustees, a nominee company or incorporation of the governing body.

A custodian trustee is a corporate body authorised to hold investments or land on behalf of others, for which they make a charge. They only act as the nominated holder and do not manage or take over the liabilities. The investments belong to the charity and the trustees are responsible for them. The charity trustees have to instruct the custodian trustee before the latter can take any action in respect of the investments.

The Official Custodian for Charities

This was a free service established under the 1960 Charities Act, which was vastly reduced under the 1993 Charities Act. The official custodian used to hold investments on behalf of charity trustees, receive and pay dividends to trustees gross of tax, inform trustees about rights issues and so on. The official custodian was not an investment adviser, however. Under the Charities Act 1993, the official custodian passed back all holdings in stocks and shares to the charity trustees themselves.

The official custodian may still hold land on behalf of charities (although there may be a charge for doing so in future) and will hold other investments in certain circumstances, for example where it is considered that the charity's property needs to be protected.

Nominee Companies

Investment managers frequently have nominee companies for holding the legal title to investments for their charity clients. Charities may only take advantage of this service if their trust deed or constitution expressly allows it, or if the Charity Commission makes an order authorising it.

Incorporation of the Governing Body

Although the trust or organisation remains unincorporated, the trustee body is incorporated and may therefore hold the title to investments. This avoids the situation where individual trustees have to put their names forward for the purposes of holding investments or executing other legal documents.

Summary

Trustees need to consider their investment policy and strategy very carefully, taking advice where appropriate. Investment strategies will vary depending on the amount available to the charity to invest, but small charities should still consider their policy in this area, as they still have a duty to maximise the return on the charity's assets.

SECTION 2

ACCOUNTS AND AUDIT

Chapter 5

ACCOUNTING BASICS

ACCOUNTING RECORDS

Good financial records are the basis for good financial management of your organisation. All organisations need to keep records of their transactions so that they can access information about the financial position. This information is retrospective, but keeping good records will help you to plan the future better. It is worth spending some time thinking about the information you will need, so that you can keep your records in sufficient detail. You need to know how much the organisation has received over a specific time period, but you also need to know what sort of income it was and the sources. This information can then be used, for example, to determine the effectiveness of a fundraising strategy.

Legal Requirements for Accounting Records

All charities are required by law to keep adequate accounting records. Section 41 of the Charities Act 1993 extends the provisions set out in the Charities Act 1960 in relation to the maintenance of accounting records.

◆ Charities must keep accounting records to show and explain the charity's transactions.
◆ The accounting records should contain day to day entries for all sums of money received or spent, showing the source or destination of funds.
◆ Charities must keep records of assets and liabilities.
◆ Trustees should be able to show with reasonable accuracy the charity's financial position on any particular date in the past.
◆ Accounting records must be kept for at least six years after the end of the financial year to which they relate.

The above applies to all unincorporated charities; charitable companies are covered by similar requirements in company legislation.

Simple Accounting Records

If the charity is small, then there is no need to keep complicated books. For many charities, an analysed cash book will be quite adequate as the main accounting record. This is a simple, day by day record of receipts and payments analysed under various headings. The headings should coincide with the budget headings, for example rent, postage, stationery (see example analysed cash book on pp87-88). A straightforward filing system can support the entries made in the book – a lever arch file for payments, with invoices filed in cheque number order is sufficient. A folder for holding invoices awaiting payment would deal with creditors. Similarly, good filing systems can deal with controls needed for receipts.

Minimum Accounting Records

At the very least, every charity should have the following:

- cash book for each bank account (for example current and deposit accounts)

- file for paid invoices, keeping them in date order of payment, marking on them date paid, cheque number and by whom approved

- folder for unpaid invoices

- file for income related correspondence or remittance advices

- filing systems for correspondence relating to grants and donations from regular funders

- petty cash book

- file or envelopes for petty cash vouchers

Keeping Accounts Records

The Cash book

The cash book records all the transactions going through the bank account. If you have more than one bank account, you should keep separate cash books for each. The purpose of the book is to keep a record of all the transactions going through the bank in greater detail than the bank statement will provide, and to identify at any time the balance of money in the bank. It is also used to analyse the receipts and payments into appropriate headings.

When purchasing a cash book you should ensure that it is ruled and has plenty of columns for all the different categories of income and expenditure that your organisation has.

Receipts (taken from the paying in book) are usually written on the left-hand side and the details recorded as follows:
◆ Date
◆ Reference (e.g. paying in slip no.)
◆ Payee
◆ Amount – in total
◆ Amount – analysed under the appropriate heading.

Payments (taken from the cheque book stubs) are normally written on the right hand side in cheque number order. Standing orders may be entered from standing order forms (it is a good idea to have a master list of all your standing orders showing frequency, amount and payee).

Bank reconciliation

The cash book must be kept up to date and reconciled regularly to the bank statements to ensure that the organisation's records are complete and accurate. The bank reconciliation will also highlight any errors made by the bank. If bank reconciliations are performed at the end of each month then the cash book will be an accurate, complete and up-to-date record of all receipts and payments. A sample form is included in this chapter on page 91.

Bank reconciliations are normally performed monthly, as follows:
◆ obtain bank statement for period
◆ check items from cash book and tick off against bank statement
◆ enter bank statement balance at end of month
◆ list payments not yet presented (i.e. not yet cleared on the bank statement)
◆ list income not yet credited
◆ calculate corrected bank balance
◆ enter in the cash book any items of expenditure on the bank statement not already in the cash book (e.g. standing orders, bank charges)
◆ enter in the cash book any items of income on the bank statement not already in the cash book (e.g. direct credits, bank interest)
◆ enter cash book balance at end of previous month
◆ enter total receipts and payments for the month
◆ calculate balance according to cash book.

Petty Cash Book

The Petty Cash Book records all the transactions going through the petty cash tin. If your organisation has more than one centre, you may wish to provide more than one petty cash tin, and a petty cash book should be kept for each.

The cash going into the tin should always come from the bank, i.e. you go to the bank and draw on a cheque. If you receive cash it should be banked intact and not put into the petty cash tin. This is very important because it ensures that a proper control over cash is exercised.

You should decide on an amount for the petty cash float, say £50 or £100, depending on the expected level of expenditure.

The Imprest System

Having drawn an initial cheque for cash of say £100, all subsequent amounts drawn should equal the amount of expenditure and therefore top up the float so that it consists of £100 cash again. When people draw money from the petty cash tin they should use petty cash vouchers. Effectively, the cash to top up should always be exchanged for vouchers to the same value. This is the imprest system.

An advantage of this system is that at any time you count the money and vouchers in the tin, they should always add up to £100. If they do not, then someone may have forgotten to put in a voucher or taken the wrong change.

When you top up the float take out the old vouchers as you put the money in. The vouchers are used as the source information for writing up the Petty Cash Book and so it is essential that they are complete. Vouchers should be kept in a file.

The Petty Cash Book will look similar to the cash book but is normally smaller because the expenditure is on a few budget headings only. As in the cash book, you need to enter the total amount of the voucher in the total column and then use the columns extending to the right to analyse the expenditure under appropriate headings. When you total all the columns you have a summary of how that amount of petty cash was spent.

Non-imprest Systems

An alternative to the imprest system is to draw cash from the bank in round sums as required. Expenditure from Petty Cash is entered in the Petty Cash Book as above from the vouchers and totalled regularly (normally monthly). A control account should also be performed regularly.

Daily Banking Sheet

If the organisation receives more than a few cheques per week, then it should consider daily banking. In addition, a proper record of cash and cheques received should be made at the time the post is opened (this should be undertaken with two people present). An example sheet is included in this chapter on page 92 and this can be adapted if you only bank on a weekly basis. If this sheet is used, then the totals from the sheet can be entered into the receipts side of the cash book, rather than repeating all the same information again. This streamlines the recordkeeping and saves time. You will then need to keep the sheets in a file in date order, as they form part of the receipts record.

Expenses Claim Form

Staff and volunteers may need to be reimbursed for expenses incurred on behalf of the organisation, for example travel, accommodation or small purchases. It is better to use proper expenses claim forms (see example on page 90) for this purpose, rather than petty cash vouchers. Receipts for the expenses can be stapled to the back of the form, as evidence of the expense. This ensures that proper authorisation for these expenses is obtained, whereas using petty cash can circumvent such controls. This is important for proper administration of the payroll as well. A compliance visit from the Inland Revenue will usually include a check on petty cash, looking for cash payments to casuals, staff, volunteers. The form included in this chapter can be adapted to your own organisation and it is advisable to create separate forms for staff and volunteers, especially as the rules for reimbursement and authorisation are usually different for each of these two categories.

It is possible to pay the reimbursements out through the petty cash system, but the expenses claim form should still be used as documentation, rather than petty cash vouchers.

Full Bookkeeping Systems

Nominal Ledger

Full bookkeeping systems use a nominal ledger. This is a central record which pulls together the basic bookkeeping information. The nominal ledger is like a series of pigeon-holes, and you can use it to sort basic information. You will need to feed information from your working account books (cash book, petty cash book, sales and purchase ledgers) into the nominal ledger. It allows for records to contain information about cost centres (i.e. the different departments or projects under which the costs fall), and is therefore a better basis for preparing accounts, particularly as your organisation becomes larger or more complex. You should also consider setting up a nominal ledger when the organisation has several projects or several different funders requiring different reports. It will also help to set up appropriate systems prior to computerising accounts (see Chapter 8). The summarised information from the cash books will be entered each month.

A nominal ledger will contain a page for each account heading (rent, stationery, equipment, salaries, telephone etc.), and should include all the different types of receipts and payments, as well as assets and liabilities. It is similar to a card index system; in effect, when you write up the nominal ledger from the cash books or other day books, you are sorting information into appropriate pigeon holes.

Other elements in a full bookkeeping system may include:
◆ Sales ledger and sales day book
◆ Purchase ledger and purchase day book
◆ Stock ledger.

These, together with the cash books are the day to day working accounts books.

It is quite possible to set up a nominal ledger without these additional ledgers; the choice will depend on the activities of your organisation. If you have a significant amount of sales on credit, then you will need to keep track of the amounts owed to the organisation, so a sales ledger is advisable. In a similar way, the decision to set up a purchase ledger will depend on the volume of purchase invoices. A purchase ledger is not necessary if you only have a few purchases and usually pay these promptly. If you can manage with just a folder for unpaid invoices, then this is probably quite adequate.

Having completed all the entries for a particular time period, it is possible to list all the balances on each account. This is known as a trial balance and it is the starting point for the preparation of accounts if you keep a nominal ledger. From the trial balance you will need to sort the balances into those which are assets, liabilities, incoming or expended resources. You then make the adjustments for accruals, prepayments, depreciation and so on, as described below.

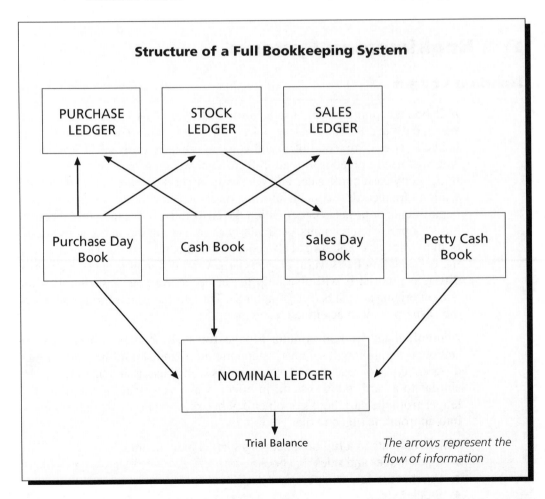

Structure of a Full Bookkeeping System

PURCHASE LEDGER

STOCK LEDGER

SALES LEDGER

Purchase Day Book

Cash Book

Sales Day Book

Petty Cash Book

NOMINAL LEDGER

Trial Balance

The arrows represent the flow of information

Preparing Accounts

Accounts need to take into consideration not only the receipts and payments for a particular period, but also the assets and liabilities. Adjustments will also have to be made to reflect any outstanding unpaid bills and pre-paid expenses at the end of the financial year. Receipts and payments will be the starting point for the preparation of accounts, but you will need to make the necessary adjustments so that your final statement of financial activities shows the picture for the whole year. The adjustments are the loose ends which will be incorporated into the end of year balance sheet and picked up at the beginning of the next financial year.

If you do not keep a nominal ledger the accounts preparation process can be done from the cash books.

Accruals and Prepayments

To ensure that the accounts reflect the actual incoming resources and expenditure for a particular time period, adjustments have to be made to allow for timing differences between the cash transaction and the financial period it should belong to. It is for this reason that the accounts will not always reflect the cash book totals for the financial year. The preparation of accounts starts with the receipts and payments but then adjusts those amounts to produce incoming resources and expenditure, matching up accruals and prepayments into the correct financial years.

Accrual – example

Your financial year ends on 31st March. In May you receive an electricity bill for £450 which covers three months use from 2nd February to 1st May. One month's usage is estimated at £150. February and March usage should be included in the accounts for the financial year to 31st March, so an accrual (i.e. a record of the debt) for electricity of £300 needs to be included in the costs for the financial year ending 31st March.

Prepayment – example

Your financial year ends on 30th June, but you have paid an insurance premium of £900 for one year's cover on 15th April. By 30th June, you have only 'used up' two and a half months of the premium, so only that proportion (i.e. 2.5 ÷ 12 x £900 = £187.50) should be included as a cost in the accounts up to 30th June.

The rest of the payment is carried forward to the following financial year as a prepayment.

Stock is another form of prepayment because you have bought something in advance of using it.

Accruals and prepayments are collected up and all go into the balance sheet. Prepayments are listed as assets because some future benefit will come from them; accruals are listed as liabilities because you have used a service but not yet paid for it.

Where to look for accruals	Where to look for prepayments
Rent	Insurance
Rates	Computer Maintenance
Electricity	Rent
Gas	Rates
Telephone	Subscriptions
Audit Fees	Training

Depreciation

Depreciation is a way of recognising that fixed assets such as equipment do lose value and suffer wear and tear. This is another cost to the organisation which needs to be accounted for. It can only be estimated, hence you will need to explain how depreciation is estimated in your notes to the accounts. In this way, readers of accounts can come to their own conclusions about whether the basis of the estimate is reasonable or not.

Depreciation – example 1

Your organisation is expanding and opening a shop to sell bought-in goods to visitors. The cost of fitting out the shop is £10,000. This money has been spent in anticipation that it will help to produce future income. You will need to estimate how long you think the equipment will last and therefore how long it will generate income for. If you estimate this period to be five years, then the depreciation is £10,000 over five years = £2,000 a year.

In other words the estimated cost of the wear and tear on the equipment and shop fittings is £2,000 a year over five years. This is more reasonable than trying to recover the whole cost of fitting out the shop in year one.

Depreciation is allowed on fixed assets such as equipment and vehicles. The actual purchase cost of such items is treated differently to other payments, for example bills, salaries and rent. Expenditure on fixed assets is separated out and put into the balance sheet. It will not appear as a single cost on your Statement of Financial Activities, instead the yearly depreciation cost appears in the SoFA over several years.

Depreciation – example 2

Your organisation buys a minibus which is used to transport elderly people on visits to day centres. The minibus cost £8,000 and you estimate that it will have a useful life of four years. Its yearly depreciation will be £2,000. This will appear in the balance sheet as:

End of Year 1 (Extract)	£		End of Year 2 (Extract)	£
Fixed Asset - cost	8,000		Fixed Asset - cost	8,000
Depreciation to date	(2,000)		Depreciation to date	(4,000)
Net Book Value	6,000		Net Book Value	4,000

End of Year 3 (Extract)	£		End of Year 4 (Extract)	£
Fixed Asset - cost	8,000		Fixed Asset - cost	8,000
Depreciation to date	(6,000)		Depreciation to date	(8,000)
Net Book Value	2,000		Net Book Value	Nil

Depreciation for each year appears as an expenditure item, as well as reducing the value of the fixed assets.

At the end of an asset's estimated useful life it will have a nil net book value. This does not necessarily mean that it is unusable, simply that further use is a bonus. If the estimated useful life of an asset changes, you could consider changing the yearly depreciation, however this is not necessary unless the effect on the accounts is significant.

Accounting for Gifts in Kind

Donated equipment should be included in the accounts by showing the value to the charity under 'donations'. The same amount will then be treated as a fixed asset and depreciated accordingly. It is in effect as if someone had given you the cash and you had bought the asset. In a similar way, any donated goods should be brought into the accounts. However, charities selling donated goods in shops will only need to record the proceeds of the sale as a donation, rather than having to value the goods. Also, charities receiving donated goods for distribution usually only bring these into the accounts at the time of distribution.

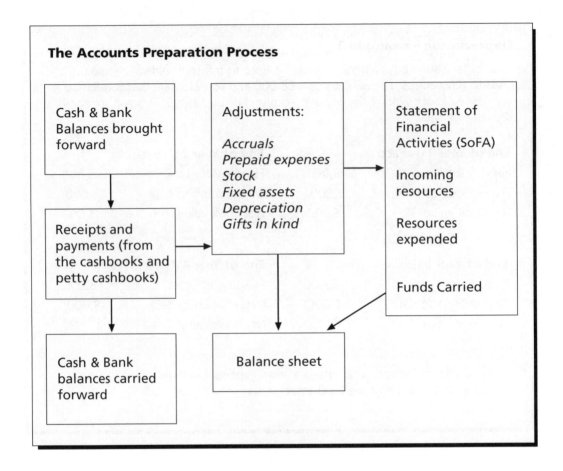

The Accounts Preparation Process

- Cash & Bank Balances brought forward
- Receipts and payments (from the cashbooks and petty cashbooks)
- Cash & Bank balances carried forward

Adjustments:

Accruals
Prepaid expenses
Stock
Fixed assets
Depreciation
Gifts in kind

Statement of Financial Activities (SoFA)

Incoming resources

Resources expended

Funds Carried

Balance sheet

Summary

Good accounting records will help in the good management of the organisation. Those records will need to become more extensive as the organisation grows, and will need to cope with the complex funding of most charities. Bookkeeping involves the maintenance of the accounts records, which may include a nominal ledger and other ledgers. Accounts preparation is more than bookkeeping, being the preparation of a statement of financial activities and balance sheet, taking into account the various adjustments needed.

Example - Cash Book Receipts

Date	Source	Ref	Total £	Fees £	M'ship £	Donations £	Grants £	Other £	Notes
April 1st	Local Authority	R/345	25,000.00				25,000.00		
April 3rd	Whitbread	R/346	2,000.00			2,000.00			
April 3rd	Collection	R/347	3,089.45			3,089.45			
April 4th	April membership	R/348	4,050.00		4,050.00				
April 6th	Insurance claim	R/349	1,018.76					1,018.76	
April 13th	XYZ - Consultancy	R/350	500.00	500.00					
April 15th	BT Community Fund	R/351	1,000.00			1,000.00			
April 17th	Refund - training fee	R/352	105.00					105.00	
April 20th	Anonymous donation	R/353	100.00			100.00			
April 24th	Sponsored Swim	R/354	756.42			756.42			
April 28th	BBC appearance fee	R/355	70.00	70.00					
		TOTAL	37,689.63	570.00	4,050.00	6,945.87	25,000.00	1,123.76	

Example - Cash Book Payments

Date	Source	Ref	Total £	Salaries £	Tel/fax Post £	Stat'y £	Rent £	Training£	Subs £	Sundry £	Travel £
1/4	Landlord - rent	Chq 367	2,345.00				2,345.00				
1/4	Voluntary Service Council	Chq 368	70.00					70.00			
3/4	Stamps	Chq 369	100.00		100.00						
4/4	DSC	Chq 370	110.00		110.00						
5/4	Local Authority - rates	D/D	93.80				93.80				
8/4	Dudley	Chq 371	264.92			264.92					
15/4	British Telecom	Chq 372	458.03		458.03						
18/4	Inland Revenue	Chq 373	2,964.84	2,964.84							
20/4	Net Pay	BACS	6,917.96	6,917.96							
22/4	Petty Cash	Chq 374	97.64		15.00	3.45			35.00	44.19	
25/4	Legal & General	Chq 375	960.35							960.35	
26/4	Staff Expenses	BACS	306.42			21.15			14.00	23.75	247.52
30/4	British Telecom - Fax	Chq 376	108.92		108.92						
	TOTAL		**14,797.88**	**9,882.80**	**791.95**	**289.52**	**2,438.80**	**70.00**	**49.00**	**1,028.29**	**247.52**

Example - Petty Cash Book

RECEIPTS

Date	Cheque	Amount
22/4	Chq 374	97.64
TOTAL		**97.64**

PAYMENTS

Date	Details	Voucher	Total £	Postage £	Stat'y £	Pubs £	Provisions £	Cleaning £
2/4	Stamps	PCV143	5.00	5.00				
3/4	Folders	PVC144	1.23		1.23			
4/4	Milk	PCV145	6.70				6.70	
6/4	Cleaning Materials	PCV146	3.67					3.67
8/4	Reference Book	PCV147	35.00			35.00		
11/4	Milk	PCV148	6.70				6.70	
13/4	Stamps	PCV149	5.00	5.00				
15/4	Tape	PCV150	2.22		2.22			
18/4	Milk	PCV151	6.70				6.70	
19/4	Cleaning Materials	PCV152	7.84					7.84
20/4	Tea, Coffee etc.	PCV153	5.88				5.88	
21/4	Milk	PCV154	6.70				6.70	
22/4	Stamps	PCV155	5.00	5.00				
TOTAL			**97.64**	**15.00**	**3.45**	**35.00**	**32.68**	**11.51**

Example - Expenses Claim Form

Name.. Month..

Date	Reason/Nature of Expense	Total	Travel	Stat'y	Sub/Pub	Provisions	Other
TOTAL							

Claimed by...

Approved..(Signature)

Date............

Example - Bank Reconciliation

Adjustments to Bank Statement Balance

Balance per bank statement at................(date)	£	
Less: Unpresented cheques		
Cheque no.		
TOTAL	**£**	
Plus: Outstanding credits	£	
Pay in Slip no.		
TOTAL	**£**	

Adjusted Bank Balance

	£
(These adjustments will clear next month)	

Adjustments to Cash Book Balance

Balance brought forward in Cash Book	£	
Plus: Receipts in Month	£	+
Less: Payments in Month	£	–
Balance carried forward	£	
Less: expenditure on bank statement, not in Cash Book	£	
(For example, bank charges)		
TOTAL	**£**	
Plus: income on bank statement, not in Cash Book	£	
TOTAL	**£**	

Adjusted Cash Book Balance

	£
(Write these adjustments into your Cash Book)	

Prepared by... Date..........

Example - Daily Banking Sheet

Analysis

Chq/Csh	Received from	Receipt No.	£	Grants	Donations	Subs	Other
	TOTAL						

PAYING IN SLIP NO...........................PAID IN TO BANK BY ....

Initials................Date...............................

ENTERED NOMINAL LEDGER... ....

Initials................Date...............................

Chapter 6

CHARITY ANNUAL ACCOUNTS AND AUDIT

The Charities Act 1993 provides the legal framework for the audit and accounts of unincorporated charities. Charitable companies should refer to Companies Act legislation for determining whether a statutory audit is required or not. There are special provisions for small charities and again these vary depending on whether the charity is a company or not. The format of the accounts for all charities is guided by *The Statement of Recommended Practice: Accounting by Charities* (SORP) issued by the Charity Commission in conjunction with the Accounting Standards Board.

THE FORM OF CHARITY ACCOUNTS

The Statement of Recommended Practice: Accounting by Charities (SORP) was introduced in October 1995 and a revised version (called Accounting and Reporting by Charities) was issued in October 2000. This is commonly referred to as SORP 2000. The revised version applies to accounting periods commencing on or after 1 January 2001. It contains guidance on the suitable treatment and presentation of charity accounts and represents good practice. The SORP applies to all charities, except for very small charities and a few instances where there is more specialised SORP, such as higher education institutions and registered social landlords. The most important points in the SORP are explained below.

No Profit

The SORP tries to get away from the concept of profit as the measure of success or failure. The profit concept is not appropriate to charities, as charity law requires them to use all funds to further the charitable objects. The profit and loss account (income and expenditure account) is therefore replaced by a Statement of Financial Activities (SoFA). The SoFA brings together all the resources available to the charity and shows how these have been used to fulfil the charity's objectives.

Incoming Resources

Charities should show all incoming resources under suitable headings in the accounts in the year in which they arise under suitable catagories. The SORP requires incoming resources to be shown in the following catagories:

- donations, legacies and similar incoming resources
- incoming resources from the operating activities of the charity, separating two main areas:
  1. activities in furtherance of the charity's objects
  2. activities for generating funds
- investment income (including bank interest)
- other incoming resources.

Charities may use headings that are appropriate to describe their activities, so it is not obligatory to use the exact words of those heading. However, it is necessary to reflect the split between those key areas. Charities are encouraged to use sub-headings to describe the activities generating incoming funds in more detail. It is common practice for the details of sources of funding to be included in the notes to the accounts, for example details of grant funders.

Resources Expended

Normal accounting concepts apply to the recognition of expenditure for charities, with expenditure incurred before the end of the financial year included in the resources expended for that financial year. The SORP catagories of expenditure are:

1. Costs of generating funds

2. Charitable expenditure:
- grants payable in furtherance of the charity's objects
- costs of activities in furtherance of the charity's objects
- support costs
- management and administration of the charity.

Costs of Generating Funds

The costs of generating funds are the costs of obtaining funds for the charity's work, such as advertising, direct mail, staff time, agent's fees. It can include obtaining donations, but also sales of goods or services if the purpose is to raise funds, for example the sale of Christmas cards. It will also include negotiating contracts or bids for new work, although the cost of monitoring and reporting progress on such contracts would usually be seen as part of the support costs of the work funded by the contract.

Publicity to raise the charity's profile should be included in this category, but not advertising to promote the charity's objects or to educate people about the cause. For example, advertising to recruit volunteers or new pupils to a school should be see as part of the charitable activities of the charity. Advertising a jumble sale to raise funds would be part of the costs of generating funds. Publicity to promote the charity's objects is likely to be targeted at beneficiaries or others who can use the information to further the charity's objectives.

Information targeted at potential donors (rather than potential beneficiaries) should be part of the costs of generating funds, even where it provides general information about the charity's activities.

Fundraising costs should not be netted off against income. Where a subsidiary company is used to undertake some of the charity's fundraising activities, the costs of those activities would have to be included under the costs of generating funds in the consolidated SoFA.

Investment management fees are included under the costs of generating funds.

Charitable Expenditure

Charitable expenditure comprises all expenditure directly relating to the objects of the charity. It should include grants payable and the direct cost of supporting charitable activities and projects (for example salaries, office, communications and other costs identifiable as an integral part of the cost of carrying out those charitable activities or projects), as well as depreciation of fixed assets where used wholly or mainly for charitable activities. The charity should describe the main charitable activities and attribute expenditure to them to give an indication of the way resources are expended. This should mirror the activities shown under the incoming resources catagories as far as possible. A note to the accounts will give further analysis of the expenditure.

Support Costs

Support costs are part of the charitable expenditure and may be the management of projects from a central office. Support costs may be identified to the charity's activities as an integral part of the cost of providing those services. However, if significant, support costs should be shown separately on the face of the SoFA.

Management and Administration of the Charity

The costs of managing and administering the charity will include direct costs incurred in organisational administration and complying with statutory requirements. For example, the cost of audit and trustees' meetings would be management and administration of the charity. However, there will also be some staff time and office costs which should be apportioned to this catagory. Note that the management of the charity's projects is a charitable expense, which will usually be treated as a support cost.

As well as showing the expenditure under these headings on the face of the SoFA, you need to describe the expenditure in 'natural' headings in the notes to the accounts. These are the catagories of rent, rates, salaries, etc. that we are accustomed to in ordinary accounts. The notes should also show how the totals on the SoFA are constituted.

Fund Accounting

One of the other major changes to the format of charity accounts is that all incoming and outgoing resources, assets and liabilities belong to a fund in the charity's accounts. It is necessary to track funds through the accounts, so that one knows the amounts received and expended and the balances on each type of fund. The different types of funds are as follows.

◆ *Permanent Endowment Funds* are donations that have been given to a charity to be held as capital with no power to convert the funds to income. These may be cash or other assets.
◆ *Expendable Endowment Funds* are donations that have been given to a charity to be held as capital, where the trustees do have a discretionary power to use the funds as income.
◆ *Restricted Funds* are funds subject to special trusts specified by the donor. This might be because it was a public appeal for a specific purpose, grants or donations. It may also include land, buildings or other assets donated to a charity. The trustees will be in breach of trust if they use restricted income other than for the specified purpose. Interest or other investment income on a restricted fund will usually be added to the fund. In some cases the terms of the donation will state how investment income should be applied. The various restricted funds may be grouped together, but should be separately disclosed in the notes to the accounts if significant.
◆ *Unrestricted Funds* are funds available for the purposes of the charity, to be spent as the trustees see fit.
◆ *Designated Funds* are unrestricted funds that have been earmarked for a particular purpose by the trustees. The notes to the accounts should explain the purpose of designated funds.
◆ *General Funds* are unrestricted funds which have not been earmarked and may be used generally to further the charity's objects.

Other Requirements of the SORP

The SORP sets out how certain areas should be handled for the purposes of charity accounting. These are looked at in detail in *A Practical Guide to Charity Accounting* (Directory of Social Change, 2002) and therefore only the most important points are mentioned here in checklist form.

- ◆ Gifts in kind are assets donated to the charity, which should be included at their value to the charity both as a donation and an asset.
- ◆ Intangible income relates to the services donated to the charity, which should be included if the donor has to bear the cost of providing the service. Include under donations and the relevant expense heading.
- ◆ Volunteer help should not normally be included unless it is intangible income. Usually it is adequate to explain in the trustees' annual report how volunteers contribute to the work of the charity.
- ◆ Investments should be revalued to market value at each balance sheet date, with unrealised gains and losses shown in the SoFA under the appropriate fund heading.
- ◆ All incoming resources received and receivable should be included in the SoFA, including legacies and new endowments.
- ◆ Funds for the purchase of fixed assets are included as restricted income, with the related depreciation being charged to the fund, thus reducing it over the life of the related assets.

Annual Accounting Requirements of Charities

The annual accounting requirements of unincorporated charities are set out in Part VI of the Charities Act 1993 and the Accounts and Reports Regulations 1995 and 2000. Charitable companies follow the company legislation (see below).

Charities must prepare accounts in the correct format for each financial year and submit them to the Charity Commission within ten months of the end of the financial year. The basic requirements are that larger charities must prepare a Statement of Financial Activities (SoFA) and a balance sheet. The accounting regulations also specify the need for explanatory notes – which must accompany the accounts – and the categories in which items should be shown in the main statements. There are some exceptions from the requirements for smaller unincorporated charities.

Charities Not Exceeding the £100,000 Threshold

Unincorporated charities with gross income of not more than £100,000 may choose to prepare a simpler form of accounts comprising a receipts and payments account, accompanied by a statement of assets and liabilities. This will be instead of the SoFA and balance sheet. There is no prescribed format set out in the regulations, but the Charity Commission have produced practical guidance with example accounts in their guide *CC64 SORP 2000: Receipts and Payments Accounts Pack*.

These smaller charities may choose to prepare accounts under the accruals basis if they wish, but if they do, then they must comply with the requirements of the accounting regulations and follow the recommendations of the SORP. Accruals accounts must consist of a SoFA and balance sheet. The SORP recommends that charities describe expenditure by activity and then give details of the breakdown into the normal expense-type headings in the notes to the accounts. However, under the accounting regulations, smaller charities may simplify the description of their expenditure in the SoFA. This means that they may use the normal expense-type headings they may have used in their old income and expenditure account, i.e. salaries, rent, rates, light, heat and so on. This means that the SoFA for many smaller charities will not be very different to an income and expenditure account. Further guidance for these charities is available from the Charity Commission in *CC65 SORP: Accruals Accounts Pack*.

Charities Not Exceeding the £10,000 Threshold

Even smaller charities with neither gross income nor total expenditure exceeding £10,000 have to prepare accounts, but do not have to submit them to the Charity Commission unless requested to do so. In the case of unincorporated charities, these may be on the receipts and payments basis or accruals basis.

Exempt Charities

These are certain categories of charities which are exempt from registration with the Charity Commission and the sections of the Charities Act relating to accounts and audit. In practice these charitable bodies are usually already subject to specific provisions relating to their accounts and audit under other regulatory bodies. Exempt charities are listed in Schedule 2 to the Charities Act 1993.

The accounts of these charities should follow the SORP, unless a more specific SORP applies, such as for universities and housing associations.

Excepted Charities

These are certain categories of charities which do not have to register with the Charity Commission, although they may register if they wish. If they do register, then they must send in their annual report and accounts to the Charity Commission. However, if they are not registered, then they do not need to submit reports and accounts. The trustees still have a statutory duty to prepare annual accounts and they have to comply with other requirements, such as sending their accounts to a member of the public if requested to do so.

Charitable Companies

The relevant sections of the Charities Act 1993 (sections 41-44), and accounting regulations 3-9 concerning the form and content of accounts, do not apply to charitable companies. They are required to prepare accounts in the form prescribed by the Companies Acts and these accounts must show a true and fair view. In order to comply with the requirement to show a true and fair view, charitable companies will be expected to comply with the SORP. In practice, therefore, the format of their accounts should be very similar to that of unincorporated charities, although certain charitable companies may need to prepare a Summary Income and Expenditure Account as well as a SoFA. It does mean that charitable companies cannot opt for the receipts and payments basis; all accounts of companies must be prepared under the accruals basis and must be submitted to Companies House within ten months of the financial year end. (Note: there are penalties for the late submission of accounts to Companies House, which start at £100 for accounts up to three months late, rise to £250 for accounts filed three to six months late, £500 for accounts filed six to twelve months late, and £1,000 for accounts filed more than twelve months late.)

Charity Commission Filing

Apart from the small charities up to the £10,000 threshold, all registered charities, including charitable companies, must submit their annual report and accounts to the Charity Commission within ten months of the financial year end. In addition, the Charity Commission ask charities to submit a completed annual return for the year and a database update form. The information required on the annual return will include extracts from the accounts, so it may be easier to complete these all at the same time.

Charity annual reports and accounts are available for public inspection at the Charity Commission offices.

In addition, members of the public may request a copy of the latest annual accounts of the charity and the charity must send them within two months. The charity may charge a reasonable fee for doing so, such as for photocopying and postage.

Audit Requirements

Prior to the Charities Act 1993, unincorporated charities were not required by statute to have an audit, although the trust deed or constitution may have set out an audit requirement, or it may have been a condition of certain funders. Section 43 of the Charities Act 1993 requires larger charities to have an audit for financial years commencing on or after 1 March 1996. This part of the Charities Act 1993 does not apply to charitable companies, as the audit regime for companies is already set out in the Companies Acts.

Larger charities are those with gross income or total expenditure exceeding £250,000 and they must be audited by a registered auditor. A registered auditor is one who is qualified to undertake audits of companies and is regulated in his or her work. If a large charity's gross income and total expenditure drops below the threshold of £250,000, it must continue to have a professional audit for a further two years.

Independent Examination

Smaller charities, that is those with gross income and total expenditure not exceeding £250,000, may instead have an independent examination. This is a type of external examination brought in by the Charities Act 1993 which may be undertaken by anyone with experience of accounting, but who does not have to be a qualified accountant or auditor. Detailed guidance on the independent examination has been issued by the Charity Commission in *CC*

Accounting and Audit Requirements

Unincorporated Charities	*Accounts*	*External Scrutiny*
Gross income over £250,000	Accruals basis following SORP	Audit by registered auditor
£100,000 - £250,000	Accruals basis following SORP	Independent examination
£10,000 - £100,000	Receipts and Payments Account and Statement of Assets and Liabilities	Independent examination
Less than £10,000	Receipts and Payments basis - no need to submit to CC	No external scrutiny required by statute
Charitable Companies	*Accounts*	*External Scrutiny*
Gross income over £250,000	Accruals basis following SORP	Audit by registered auditor
£90,000 - £250,000	Accruals basis following SORP	Compilation report
Less than £90,000	Accruals basis following SORP	No external scrutiny required

63 Examination of Charity Accounts 2001: Directions and Guidance Notes. Charities in this category may choose to have an audit, if the trustees think it is wise or if they have relatively complex affairs. It will be necessary to have an audit if the constitution requires it or if it is required by funders.

Small charities, that is those with gross income and total expenditure not exceeding £10,000, do not need to have a statutory audit or an independent examination, but they must check their constitution and their funders' requirements.

Smaller and very small charities may need to contact the Charity Commission for advice on how the constitution may be amended so that they can take advantage of the reliefs from audit.

Audit of Charitable Companies

Larger charitable companies are required to have an audit by a registered auditor. Charitable companies with gross income below £250,000 and net assets of less than £1.4 million may opt to have a compilation report instead of an audit.

Companies with a gross income of up to £90,000 and a balance sheet total less than £1.4 million are not required to have an audit or a compilation report.

All companies must prepare full accruals accounts and submit accounts to Companies House within ten months of the end of the year. In addition, 10% of the membership can request that an audit be performed, even if the company otherwise qualifies for the exemption.

There is no rule about the audit requirement continuing as there is for unincorporated charities; the test is applied to the current year only.

Compilation Report

A compilation report is independent confirmation that the accounts have been properly prepared from the accounting records. It does not seek to confirm that the accounting records themselves are complete and accurate. An accountant will often prepare the accounts as well, although they could just review the accounts and compare them with the underlying records. The accountant ensures that the accounts are presented properly and disclose all the information required under the Companies Acts. He or she then reports under an Accountant's Report confirming that the accounts have been properly prepared.

Annual Report

As well as annual accounts, registered charities (and excepted charities if requested) must prepare an annual report, which has to be submitted to the Charity Commission together with the accounts. This requirement applies to charitable companies as well as unincorporated charities. However, companies may incorporate the information required under the Companies Act for the directors' report into the trustees' annual report.

Very small charities with gross income or total expenditure not exceeding £10,000 do not have to prepare and file an annual report. Charities with gross income or total expenditure exceeding £250,000 have to provide a fuller report. The detailed requirements are contained in *The Charities (Accounts and Reports) Regulations 2000* and the SORP.

Requirements for Annual Reports of All Charities

- The financial year to which the report relates.
- Legal and administrative details (see below).
- A brief summary of the main activities and achievments of the charity during the year in relation to the charity's objects.
- Reserves policy.
- Investment policy.
- Grant-making policy.
- Relationships with other charities or organisations with which the charity cooperates to achieve its objectives.
- Date the report is approved, with the signature of at least one trustee who is authorised to sign on behalf of the trustees.

The legal and administrative details may be put onto one page before the narrative section of the trustees' annual report.

Legal and Administrative Details to be Included in Annual Report

- The name of the charity as it appears in the register of charities and any other name by which it makes itself known.
- The charity registration number and company number.
- Principal address of the charity and registered office of a company.
- Details of governing instrument such as the nature of the document and date established.
- Objects of the charity.
- Details of any restrictions imposed by governing document.
- A summary of any specific investment powers and their authority (for example governing document or Charity Commission order).
- Names of advisers, such as investment managers, bankers, solicitors, auditors.

- Names of trustees during the year and at the date the report is signed (or a minimum of 50 trustees if there are more than 50 trustees).
- The method by which trustees are appointed.
- The name of any other person or body entitled to appoint one or more of the charity trustees.
- The name of any other person holding property on behalf of the charity i.e. acting as a trustee.

The trustees are all responsible for the annual report and therefore it should be approved at a normal trustees' meeting, following the procedure of the charity for such matters.

Larger charities (those with gross income exceeding £250,000) need to provide a fuller narrative report as well as a statement confirming that the trustees have reviewed the major risks facng the charity and established systems to mitigate those risks.

Additional Requirements for Charities with Gross Income of More Than £250,000

- A longer review of activities and strategy to replace the brief review.
- The organisational structure of the charity (for example whether it has branches).
- Commentary on significant changes, developments and achievements in the past year.
- Description of any significant events since the end of the year and any likely future developments.
- An explanation of any funds in deficit and the action taken or planned to eradicate the deficit.
- A statement confirming that the major risks to which the charity is exposed have been reviewed and systems have been established to mitigate those risks.
- As well as the investment policy, larger charities should comment on the performance of investments over the past financial year.

Summary

Charity accounts have come under increasing scrutiny from regulators, and so charities need to ensure that they follow year end procedure. In addition, however, well presented annual accounts will help charities to fundraise and make their case. Following good practice is therefore in the charity's own interest.

CHAPTER 7

INTERPRETING ACCOUNTS

Accounts give us information about the past performance of an organisation and its overall financial health. We can therefore gather information about the viability of an organisation and how well it is managed. Care is needed when interpreting financial accounts, however, as there is often too little information to come to a firm conclusion. Accounts will simply give us pointers towards the questions that need to be asked and the lines of inquiry to pursue.

Interpreting accounts requires a combination of a little technical knowledge and plenty of practice. Chapter 5 covers some of the basics of understanding accounts and the Glossary at the beginning explains much of the jargon. This chapter covers some of the more technical areas and gives you an opportunity to practise with a case study at the end of the chapter. More practice will help to develop your skill at asking the right questions.

READING ACCOUNTS

A set of charity accounts will consist of:

◆ Trustees' Report
◆ Statement of Financial Activities (SoFA)
◆ Balance Sheet
◆ Notes to the Accounts
◆ Auditor's Report or Independent Examiner's Report.

Larger or more complex charities may additionally produce a consolidated Statement of Financial Activities, a Summary Income and Expenditure account and a Cashflow Statement. Small charities taking advantage of exemptions may produce a simpler form of accounts, such as a receipts and payments account, summary of movements on the bank and cash balances, and a statement of assets and liabilities. This form of accounts gives less information, but requires less interpretation and so this is not covered in detail in this chapter. Helpful guidance on accounts for smaller charities is contained in the Charity Commission booklets CC64 and CC65.

The first thing to establish is whether you have a full set of accounts. An incomplete set will not be helpful; the notes to the accounts particularly will provide key information. You should also check that the trustees have approved the annual accounts by looking for their signature on the balance sheet. The audit report or independent examiner's report should also be signed and dated. These signatures indicate that you are looking at final approved and audited or examined accounts, not at draft accounts.

Trustees' Annual Report

The trustees' annual report is worth reading as an introduction to the accounts. A good report should highlight significant financial transactions during the year and explain the salient features of the accounts.

Statement of Financial Activities and Balance Sheet

The main financial statements are the Statement of Financial Activities (SoFA) and the balance sheet. The SoFA replaces the income and expenditure account (profit and loss account) for charities. However, note that where the charity has no endowment funds, the SoFA will be substantially the same as an income and expenditure account.

The SoFA looks back over the past, drawing together all the transactions for the period covered by the accounts, in this case a year. (It will usually be a year, unless the charity is new or changing its financial year end for some reason.) It shows the totals for resources becoming available to the charity and resources expended for that year.

The balance sheet is a snapshot of the position at the end of the financial year. (The date of the balance sheet should always coincide with the date to which the SoFA is made up.) The balance sheet indicates the level of reserves available to the charity, as well as the assets and liabilities which represent those reserves. The balance sheet straddles the end of one accounting year and the beginning of the next. It gives us important information about the financial health and viability of the organisation.

The SoFA and the balance sheet do interlink (see the examples on pp108 and 110). The lower half of the balance sheet contains information about the balances on the various funds at the end of the financial year – this is the same information at the bottom of the SoFA. This is not a coincidence, but a consequence of balancing your accounts properly. The SoFA explains the charity's transactions over the year and shows the net results. The results accumulate over time and lead to the balances in the funds of the balance sheet. These funds are represented by the assets and liabilities on the top half of the balance sheet. The total funds of a charity are always matched by the net assets.

Look in the SoFA for:

◆ Total incoming resources and size of charity

◆ Types of incoming resource available to charity

◆ What the charity spends its money on

◆ Amount spent on administration and fundraising

◆ Unspent restricted and unrestricted funds for the year and balances carried forward

Look in Balance Sheet for:

◆ Total funds available to the charity (or reserves)

◆ Assets and liabilities belonging to each fund

◆ Liquidity and charity's ability to meet its debts

◆ Funds available to charity for specific purposes as designated funds

◆ Balances on restricted funds for future expenditure

Notes to the Accounts

The notes to the accounts expand on particular lines in the SoFA and balance sheet and you should refer to the notes as you read through the main financial statements. As a charity gets more complex, so there will be more notes. There will also be more information in the notes, as it is not possible to include such details on the SoFA or balance sheet. It is therefore important to read all the notes.

The accounting policies are there to explain the methods used to make judgements about how to treat certain items. It is not possible for every organisation to adopt exactly the same approach. Although the SORP sets down certain treatments, there are several areas where the charity still has to state what the treatment is. It is good practice to explain the treatments even if these do conform to the SORP.

Example SoFA

The example SoFA (opposite) shows incoming resources and resources expended by fund, with a separate column for each fund. The SoFA is a summary and more detailed workings deal with each specific fund. The column for endowment shows that £253,000 of new endowment funds were received in the year from donations and legacies. More detail about existing and new endowment funds would have to be given in the notes to the accounts. Further down the page, we see that the endowment fund also increased by £30,000 of unrealised gains. These arise because the endowment funds are invested (see investments under fixed assets on balance sheet). At the end of the financial year, the investments must be revalued to the market value at the date of the balance sheet. The investments have increased in value, so there is a corresponding gain in the endowment fund. Because the investments have not been sold, the gain is called *unrealised*; realised gains or losses are made when investments are sold.

The charity receives restricted income from donations and other sources for the main charitable work. We can see under the resources expended section that these activities are primarily childcare work. Administration for that work is shown under support costs.

We can also see that the charity generates unrestricted income for its charitable activities. There is a corresponding expenditure for parenting classes, so the income will be the fees charged.

The net incoming resources results from subtracting total resources expended from total incoming resources. It is the rough equivalent to surplus or deficit, although this term is not appropriate in the SoFA since it includes more than income and expenditure. This example SoFA does tell us that this charity spends nearly all its incoming resources in the year, except the endowments. The funds brought forward show us the level of reserves from previous years. Since they are not high relative to overall income, this would seem to be the regular practice of this charity.

Looking at the SoFA, one can see that this charity is heavily dependent on income received for the main charitable activities, which may be grants or fees. The small amount of income it can earn in investment income from the endowment fund is available for spending on the charitable purposes.

EXAMPLE STATEMENT OF FINANCIAL ACTIVITIES

	Endowment £	Restricted £	Unrestricted £	This Year Total £	Last Year Total £
INCOMING RESOURCES					
Donations and Legacies	253,000	27,000	15,000	295,000	57,000
Acivities to further the charity's objects		257,000	295,000	552,000	534,000
Investment Income			25,000	25,000	13,000
A. Total Incoming Resources	**253,000**	**284,000**	**335,000**	**872,000**	**604,000**
RESOURCES EXPENDED					
Costs of Generating Funds Fundraising and Publicity			15,000	15,000	23,000
Activities to further the charity's objects					
Childcare Work		254,000	45,000	299,000	285,000
Parenting Classes			220,000	220,000	203,000
Support Costs		25,000	23,000	48,000	49,000
Management and Administration			31,000	31,000	29,000
B. Total Resources Expended	**0**	**279,000**	**334,000**	**613,000**	**589,000**
C. Net Incoming Resources (A-B)	**253,000**	**5,000**	**1,000**	**259,000**	**15,000**
D. Unrealised gains	30,000			30,000	22,000
E. Net Movement on Funds (C+D)	**283,000**	**5,000**	**1,000**	**289,000**	**37,000**
F. Funds Brought Forward	250,000	30,000	73,000	353,000	316,000
Funds Carried Forward (E+F)	**533,000**	**35,000**	**74,000**	**642,000**	**353,000**

Example Balance Sheet

The stock, debtors, creditors and cash at bank are the components of the working capital of this charity. These elements move through the working capital cycle to fund the cashflow. This part of the balance sheet can be likened to a snapshot of the charity. The amount shown under each category is true for that particular day. The next day, the amount shown as due under debtors could arrive and be banked. This would change the snapshot, reducing debtors and increasing cash at bank. Note that the overall current assets would not change. If some of the creditors were paid, this would reduce creditors and the amount for cash at bank. Again, note that this would not change the net current assets.

The amount of net current assets gives a good indication of the amount of working capital available. Even though the exact amounts under each category are only true for that particular day, the net current assets figure will only change with significant new transactions and indicates the level of funds available to the charity. The net current assets provide proof that the charity can manage its cashflow and meet the debts shown under creditors. Where the current assets include significant debtors, then it is better to calculate whether the cash at bank is sufficient to pay the creditors. In the example balance sheet, there is £105,000 in the bank to pay current liabilities of £94,000.

(Note: A charity that has net current liabilities is technically insolvent. It will need the support of a bank or other funder to pay the creditors. Whilst this is a difficult position to be in, a charity does not have to wind up immediately. It must however take action to improve matters and will not be able to carry on indefinitely in a position of net current liabilities. An organisation is insolvent when it cannot pay its debts and should stop all activity at that point, obtaining advice from an accountant or insolvency practitioner.

The example balance sheet shows that £213,000 is invested in fixed assets. The charity does not have this much in unrestricted funds. However, there is a 'creditor due after more than one year' of £135,000. This is a long term loan and has probably been borrowed for a fixed asset such as a building. It is likely that this is a mortgage and in a full set of accounts you would then look through the notes to the accounts, which should reveal the nature of the fixed assets and whether they have been given as security for the loan.

Note that the balance sheet value of the investments is equal to the value of the endowment fund. The charity has to keep the endowment fund intact and has probably invested it for the long term.

The overall picture is of a reasonably healthy, solvent charity. However, the reserves are low and general funds only represent 27 days of operating costs, so they would have difficulty continuing in the event of a drop in income.

EXAMPLE BALANCE SHEET

	This Year £	Last Year £
Fixed Assets		
Tangible Fixed Assets	213,000	215,000
Investments	533,000	250,000
Figure A	**746,000**	**465,000**
Current Assets		
Stock of Publications	5,000	4,000
Debtors	15,000	17,000
Bank Balances	105,000	89,000
Figure B	**125,000**	**110,000**
Current Liabilities		
Trade Creditors	15,000	10,000
Tax and National Insurance	67,000	55,000
Other Creditors and Accruals	12,000	5,000
Figure C	**94,000**	**70,000**
Net Current Assets (B-C)	***31,000***	***40,000***
D. Total Assets less Current Liabilities (A+B-C)	777,000	505,000
E. Creditors: Amounts Due after More than One Year	135,000	152,000
NET ASSETS (D-E)	***642,000***	***353,000***
Funds		
Permanent Endowment	533,000	250,000
Restricted	35,000	30,000
Unrestricted		
Designated	28,000	28,000
General	46,000	45,000
TOTAL FUNDS	***642,000***	***353,000***

CASE STUDY –
INTERPRETING ACCOUNTS

Interpret the information given in the following example charity accounts. Consider the following basic questions, but also add any information or comments. A suggested interpretation is given at the end of the chapter.

1. Do they have more assets than liabilities?
2. Do they have money in the bank?
3. Who owes them money?
4. Who do they owe money to?
5. When will they have to pay off their liabilities?
6. Are they carrying forward funds to next year?
7. Where do they get most of their income from?
8. Are they heavily dependent on one source of income?
9. What proportion of their income do they spend on staff costs?
10. What proportion of their income do they spend on fundraising and administration?

BORSETSHIRE DRUGS ADVICE CENTRE
LEGAL AND ADMINISTRATIVE DETAILS
FOR THE YEAR ENDED 31 MARCH 2002

Name: Borsetshire Drugs Advice Centre, previously the Borchester Drugs Rehabilitation Advisory Trust

Status: Charity established as a company limited by guarantee (number 1032145) on 8 August 1992; registered with the Charity Commission number 1234567.

Principal Address and Registered Office:
10 High Street
Borchester
Borsetshire
BA1 6PR

Charity Objects: The charity is established to educate people in the area of Borsetshire about the effects of all drug use.

Charity Trustees:
Mr P Archer (Chairman)
Mrs L Snell (Vice-Chairman)
Miss U Gupta (Secretary)
Mrs M Antrobus (Treasurer)
Mr N Pargeter
Mr J Woolley
Mr G Pemberton
Mrs J Aldridge

Organisational Structure: Borsetshire Drugs Advice Centre is an independent charity and the charity trustees meet four times a year to make the major policy decisions. There are three sub-committees dealing with finance, personnel and therapeutic development, all of which meet approximately every six weeks and report to the main board of trustees.

Auditors:
Biggs & Co
Registered Auditors
High Street
Borchester
BA1 8BR

BORSETSHIRE DRUGS ADVICE CENTRE TRUSTEES' REPORT FOR THE YEAR ENDED 31 MARCH 2002

The trustees present their report and the audited financial statements for the year ended 31 March 2002.

Activities and Review

The company is a charity and exists to educate people in the area of Borsetshire about the effects of all drug use and to assist those suffering from the effects of drug abuse. To achieve this object, the charity operates a number of projects.

Advice and Information

This project is based at the central office and provides help and advice to drug users, parents, teachers, social workers and others wanting to know more about the effects of drug use. Several information leaflets have been produced and these are now available in doctors' surgeries, Borsetshire Royal Infirmary and the Citizens' Advice Bureaux in the area. Individual advice is provided at drop-in times and also by special appointment. As a result of the advice service, a parents' support group has been set up on the Borchester Green Estate.

The project is funded by Borsetshire County Council and employs four members of staff. The mainstay of the service are the many volunteers who provide advice and distribute information leaflets. In the year under review, over 1,000 volunteer hours were donated and 1,200 people were assisted. The receipt of a donation from the Berrow Estate Charitable Trust has enabled us to buy a new computer and database software, which will be used to organise information and make it more easily accessible.

Outreach Work

The work of the charity of reaching out to young people who are vulnerable to falling into drug misuse continued to expand in the year under review. At the beginning of the year, we set a target to reach 150 new people and to make our other services available to them. We did not manage to reach our target as we had some difficulty in recruiting staff. New members of the team have now been appointed and we look forward to expanding this service as planned. The outreach service also runs a health clinic, a needle exchange and a launderette to alleviate the problems of those people who do not yet feel ready to change their way of life.

We work in close cooperation with Borsetshire County Council Social Services department in operating this project. We are grateful for their support and funding. In a year's time, it is planned that this service will transfer to a contract, the terms of which will be agreed in the course of this coming year.

Cafe

The contract with Borsetshire County Council to run a cafe in the centre of Borchester continues to operate successfully. All the staff working in the cafe are former drug users training in catering. On average about 75 people use the cafe each day, which is an increase of 50% compared to the attendance when it was run by the Social Services Department. The cafe still operates from the same premises owned by the County

Council, which were given a complete facelift two years ago. Now the bright and cheerful atmosphere hosts all sorts of activities, including art exhibitions, jazz evenings and other theme evenings.

Future Plans

The charity plans to continue the activities as outlined above subject to satisfactory arrangements. In addition, the trustees plan to introduce a new scheme to place rehabilitated drug users who have been through our training projects on mentoring schemes with local employers.

Reserves Policy

The trustees have established a policy whereby the unrestricted funds not committed or invested in tangible fixed assets should be between 3 and 6 months of annual running costs, which equates to £60,000–£120,000 in general funds. This would enable the charity to continue the current activities in the event of a drop in income, while the trustees considered how to replace the funding or change the activities. At present the level of reserves is £23,775 and do not therefore reach the target level. The trustees are considering ways in which the target level can be reached.

Investment Policy

Sufficient funds are retained in short term deposit accounts at any one time to ensure that the charity can meet all its liabilities. Funds available for longer term investment are few and therefore a specialised charity unit trust has been selected for all the remaining investment funds, as this provides the balance between income and capital growth the trustees require. The return on investments in the year at over 8% is considered satisfactory.

Risk Review

The trustees have undertaken their own review of the major risks to which the charity is exposed and systems have been established to mitigate those risks. Significant external risks to funding have led to the development of a stategic plan which will allow for the diversification of funding and activities. Internal risks are minimised by the implementation of procedures for authorisation of transactions and projects and to ensure consistent quality of delivery for all operational aspects of the charity. These procedures are periodically reviewed to ensure that they meet the needs of the charity.

Trustees

Those who served as trustees and company directors during the year and up to the date of this report were as follows:

Mr P Archer
Mrs L Snell
Miss U Gupta
Mrs M Antrobus
Mr N Pargeter
Mr J Woolley
Mrs S Hebden (resigned 24 September 2001)
Mr T Forrest (resigned 11 November 2001)
Mr G Pemberton (appointed 22 October 2001)
Mrs J Aldridge (appointed 14 February 2001)

No trustee has any beneficial interest in the company. All trustees are members of the charitable company and guarantee to contribute £1 in the event of a winding up. The number of guarantees at the end of the year was 8 (2001–8).

Trustees' Responsibilities

Company law requires the directors, who are also the charity trustees, to prepare financial statements for each financial year which give a true and fair view of the state of the affairs of the company and of the results of the company for that period. In preparing those financial statements, the directors are required to:

◆ select suitable accounting policies and then apply them consistently;
◆ make judgments and estimates that are reasonable and prudent;
◆ state whether applicable accounting standards have been followed, subject to any material departures disclosed and explained in the financial statements;
◆ prepare the financial statements on the going concern basis unless it is inappropriate to assume that the company will continue on that basis.

The directors are responsible for keeping proper accounting records which disclose with reasonable accuracy at any time the financial position of the company and enable it to ensure that the financial statements comply with the Companies Act 1985. They are also responsible for safeguarding the assets of the company and hence for taking reasonable steps to prevent and detect fraud and other irregularities.

Auditors

The auditors have expressed their willingness to be reappointed in accordance with section 384 of the Companies Act 1985.

Approved by the trustees on 13 September 2002

and signed on their behalf by Philip Archer (Director)

BORSETSHIRE DRUGS ADVICE CENTRE STATEMENT OF FINANCIAL ACTIVITIES FOR THE YEAR ENDED 31 MARCH 2002

	Notes	Restricted £	Unrestricted £	This year's Total £	Last year's Total £
Incoming Resources					
Activities to Further Charity's Objects	2	150,000	115,000	265,000	224,546
Donations	3	5,000	-	5,000	6,796
Investment Income		765	900	1,665	1,324
A. Total Incoming Resources		**155,765**	**115,900**	**271,665**	**232,666**
Resources Expended					
Costs of Generating Funds					
Fundraising and Publicity		-	2,562	2,562	1,893
Activities to Further Charity's Objects					
Advice and Information		68,917	-	68,917	61,756
Outreach Work		68,391	-	68,391	53,316
Cafe		-	95,842	95,842	67,606
Management and Administration		1,250	8,827	10,077	7,372
B. Total Resources Expended	**6**	**138,558**	**107,231**	**245,789**	**191,943**
C. Net Incoming Resources (A-B)		**17,207**	**8,669**	**25,876**	**40,723**
D. Unrealised Gain on Investments	8	-	762	762	202
E. Net Movement in Funds (C+D)		17,207	9,431	26,638	40,925
F. Funds at Beginning of Year		1,316	25,594	26,910	(14,015)
Funds at End of Year (E+F)	**13**	**18,523**	**35,025**	**53,548**	**26,910**

BORSETSHIRE DRUGS ADVICE CENTRE
BALANCE SHEET AS AT 31 MARCH 2002

	Notes	This Year £	Last Year £
Fixed Assets			
Tangible Fixed Assets	7	11,250	10,000
Investments	8	11,654	10,892
Figure A		**22,904**	**20,892**
Current Assets			
Debtors	9	7,835	5,628
Cash at Bank and in Hand		31,193	9,142
Figure B		**39,028**	**14,770**
C. Creditors: Amounts Falling Due Within One Year	10	8,384	8,752
D. Net Current Assets (B-C)		*30,644*	*6,018*
Net Assets (A+D)		*53,548*	*26,910*
Funds			
Unrestricted Funds			
General Funds		23,196	24,527
Revaluation Fund		1,829	1,067
Designated Funds	11	10,000	-
Restricted Funds	12	18,523	1,316
Total Funds	**13**	**53,548**	**26,910**

These financial statements were approved by the Trustees on 13 September 2002 and signed on their behalf by M. Antrobus – Treasurer

INDEPENDENT AUDITORS' REPORT TO THE MEMBERS OF BORSETSHIRE DRUGS ADVICE CENTRE

We have audited the financial statements on the attached pages, which comprise the statement of financial activities, balance sheet and related notes. These financial statements have been prepared under the historical cost convention and the accounting policies set out in the notes.

Respective Responsibilities of the Trustees and Auditors

The trustees' responsibilities for preparing the report of the trustees and the financial statements in accordance with applicable law and the United Kingdom Accounting Standards are set out in the statement of responsibilities of trustees. Our responsibility is to audit the financial statements in accordance with relevant legal and regulatory requirements and United Kingdom Auditing Standards.

We report to you our opinion as to whether the financial statements give a true and fair view and are properly prepared in accordance with the Companies Act 1985. We also report to you if, in our opinion the report of the trustees is not consistent with the financial statements, if the company has not kept proper records, if we have not received all the information and explanations we require for our audit, or if information specified by law regarding the trustees' remuneration and transactions with the charity is not disclosed.

We are not required to consider whether the statement in the report of the trustees concerning the major risks to which the charity is exposed covers all existing risks and controls, nor to form an opinion on the effectiveness of the charity's risk management and control procedures.

We read the report of the trustees and consider whether it is consistent with the audited financial statements. We consider the implications for our report if we become aware of any apparent misstatements or material inconsistencies with the financial statements. Our responsibilities do not extend to any other information.

Basis of Opinion

We conducted our audit in accordance with United Kingdom Auditing Standards issued by the Auditing Practices Board. An audit includes examination, on a test basis, of evidence relevant to the amounts and disclosures in the financial statements. It also includes an assessment of the significant estimates and judgements made by the trustees in their preparation of the financial statements, and of whether the accounting policies are appropriate to the charity's circumstances, consistently applied and properly disclosed.

We planned and performed our audit so as to obtain all information and explanations which we considered necessary in order to provide us with sufficient evidence to give reasonable assurance that the statements are free from material misstatement, whether caused by fraud or other irregularity or error. In forming our opinion we also evaluated the overall adequacy of the presentation of information in the financial statements.

Opinion

In our opinion the financial statements give a true and fair view of the state of the charitable company's affairs as at 31 March 2002, and of its incoming resources and the application of resources, including income and expenditure, in the year then ended and have been properly prepared in accordance with the Companies Act 1985.

Biggs & Co.

Registered Auditors

BORSETSHIRE DRUGS ADVICE CENTRE
NOTES TO THE ACCOUNTS FOR THE YEAR
ENDED 31 MARCH 2002

1. Accounting Policies

a) The financial statements have been prepared under the historical cost convention, as modified by the inclusion of fixed asset investments at market value, and in accordance with applicable accounting standards and follow the recommendations in *Statement of Recommended Practice: Accounting and Reporting by Charities* (SORP) issued October 2000.

b) Donations, gifts, grants and fees are included in full in the Statement of Financial Activities when receivable.

c) Resources expended are included in the Statement of Financial Activities when the costs are incurred. The direct costs of an activity are allocated to that activity. However, the cost of overall direction and administration on each activity, comprising salary and overhead costs is apportioned on the following basis of estimated staff time spent on those activities.

Fundraising and publicity	15%
Advice and information	20%
Outreach work	20%
Cafe	30%
Management and administration of the charity	15%

d) Restricted funds are to be used for specified purposes as laid down by the donor. Expenditure which meets these criteria is identified to the fund, together with a fair allocation of management and support costs.

e) Unrestricted funds are donations and other income received or generated for the objects of the charity without further specified purpose and are available as general funds.

f) Designated funds are unrestricted funds earmarked by the trustees for particular purposes.

g) Depreciation is provided on all tangible fixed assets at rates calculated to write off the cost of each asset over its estimated useful life, which in all cases is set at four years. Items are treated as fixed assets where the initial cost exceeds £500.

h) Investments held as fixed assets are revalued at mid-market value at the balance sheet date and the gain or loss taken to the Statement of Financial Activities.

2. Activities to Further Charity's Objects

	Restricted £	Unrestricted £	This Year £	Last Year £
Borsetshire County Council grants:				
Advice and Information	70,000	-	70,000	60,000
Outreach Work	80,000	0	80,000	66,132
Contract fees		95,000	95,000	80,414
Café income	–	20,000	20,000	18,000
	150,000	**115,000**	**265,000**	**224,546**

3. Donations

	Restricted £	Unrestricted £	This Year £	Last Year £
Berrow Estate Charitable Trust – for the purchase of computer equipment	5,000	–	5,000	–
For the general purposes of the charity	–	–	–	6,796
	5,000	**–**	**5,000**	**6,796**

4. Staff Costs and Numbers

Staff costs during the year were as follows:

Salaries and Wages	191,769	144,247
Social Security Costs	19,560	15,364
	211,329	**159,611**
Total emoluments paid to staff were	191,769	144,247

The average number of employees (part-time and full-time) during the year was as follows:

Chief Officer	1
Advice and Information	4
Outreach Work	4
Cafe	6
Administration and Support	1
	16

5. Trustees' Remuneration and Expenses

The trustees received no remuneration.
Five trustees were reimbursed expenses as follows:

	This Year £	Last Year £
Travel Expenses	137	164
Reimbursement of postage and stationery	29	20
	166	**184**

BORSETSHIRE DRUGS ADVICE CENTRE NOTES TO THE ACCOUNTS
FOR THE YEAR ENDED 31 MARCH 2002

6. Total Resources Expended

	Advice & Information £	Outreach Work £	Cafe £	Fundraising & Publicity £	Mgmnt & Admin £	This Year Total £	Last Year Total £
Staff Costs	64,239	60,568	82,766	1,878	1,878	211,329	159,611
Recruitment	-	1,426	1,212	-	-	2,638	2,817
Travel	324	482	396	-	166	1,368	956
Premises	1,646	3,931	5,084	-	-	10,661	10,562
Communications	594	589	1,144	589	589	3,505	3,816
Legal and Professional	-	-	-	-	1,250	1,250	2,429
Audit and Accountancy	-	-	-	-	2,000	2,000	2,800
Consultancy	-	770	2,562	-	2,336	5,668	2,825
Volunteer Expenses	1,489	-	1,428	95	-	3,012	2,791
Depreciation	625	625	1,250	-	1,250	3,750	2,500
Bank Charges	-	-	-	-	608	608	836
TOTAL	**68,917**	**68,391**	**95,842**	**2,562**	**10,077**	**245,789**	**191,943**

BORSETSHIRE DRUGS ADVICE CENTRE
NOTES TO THE ACCOUNTS FOR THE YEAR ENDED 31 MARCH 2002

---

7. Tangible Fixed Assets

	Office Equipment £
COST	
At the beginning of the year	15,000
Additions	5,000
At the end of the year	20,000
DEPRECIATION	
At the beginning of the year	5,000
Charge for Year	3,750
At the end of the year	8,750
NET BOOK VALUE	
At the end of the year	**11,250**
At the beginning of the year	**10,000**

8. Investments

	This Year £	Last Year £
Charifund Unit Trust shares at mid-market value:		
At the beginning of the year	10,892	10,690
Change in value	762	202
At the end of the year	**11,654**	**10,892**
Historical cost of investments held at the end of the year	**9,825**	**9,825**

9. Debtors

Contract Fees Receivable	6,709	4,580
Other Debtors and Prepayments	1,126	1,048
	7,835	**5,628**

10. Creditors: Amounts Falling Due Within One Year

Taxation and Social Security	4,458	3,896
Other Creditors and Accruals	3,926	4,856
	8,384	**8,752**

11. Designated Funds

The trustees have designated funds for purchase of new equipment in the cafe.

Transferred in Year and at the end of the year   **£10,000**

12.Restricted Funds

The movements on the restricted funds of the charity were as follows:

	Beginning of Year £	Incoming £	Outgoing £	End of Year £
a) Computer Equipment	–	5,000	1,250	3,750
b) Advice and Information	1,316	70,000	68,917	2,399
c) Outreach	–	80,765	68,391	12,374
	1,316	**155,765**	**138,558**	**18,523**

The balances will be carried forward and used as follows:

a) The balance will fund future depreciation charges

b) The balance will be used to continue the advice and information activity within the terms of the fund

c) The balance arose from a delay in appointing new staff and will all be utilised in the forthcoming months.

13.Analysis of Net Assets Between Funds

	Restricted Funds £	Unrestricted Funds £	Total Funds £
Fund Balances at the end of the year are represented by:			
A. Tangible Fixed Assets	3,750	7,500	11,250
B. Investments	–	11,654	11,654
C. Current Assets	17,229	21,799	39,028
D. Creditors: Amounts Falling Due Within 1 Year	(2,456)	(5,928)	(8,384)
Total Net Assets (A+B+C-D)	**18,523**	**35,025**	**53,548**
Unrealised gains included above on investments	–	**1,829**	**1,829**

Case Study – Suggested Interpretation

1. They do have more assets than liabilities. This is shown by the net assets figure of £53,548 on the balance sheet, which is the same as the total funds. The assets that are actually available to them to spend are the net current assets of £30,644, shown on the balance sheet at 'D'. They could sell the investments to raise more cash if necessary. However, some of these assets are part of the restricted funds, so they have to spend them in accordance with the terms of that funding. The Trustees' Report and note 12 to the accounts tell us that the majority of the restricted funds relate to the Outreach project which has suffered from a shortage of staff. Whilst they seem to have quite a lot of assets on the balance sheet, not very much relates to free reserves.

2. Yes, they do have money in the bank. This is found on the balance sheet, and at the end of the year they had £31,193 in the bank. This was more than was needed at the time to meet the creditors of £8,384 shown at the balance sheet at 'C'. This shows that they are managing their cash flow quite well. This is also an improvement on the previous year, when they had just £9,142 in the bank to meet creditors owed £8,752.

3. The debtors on the balance sheet are the people owing money to them. These are further explained in note 9 to the accounts. This shows that the greater part of the debtors figure is owed by the local authority on the contract fees for the cafe training project.

4. They owe money to creditors in the balance sheet of £8,384, which is further explained in note 10 to the accounts. Approximately half the creditors amount relates to outstanding tax and National Insurance; the other half relates to other creditors and accruals, probably suppliers of goods and services.

5. All the liabilities are short term – that is they are creditors due within one year (current liabilities).

6. They are carrying funds forward to the next year. This is shown in the lower half of the balance sheet and also on the last line of the SoFA. The balance sheet shows a little more detail, as this breaks down the unrestricted funds into their components. We can see that they have general funds of £23,196, which will have arisen from the surpluses over a number of years. They also have a revaluation fund of £1,829, which arises from revaluing the investments to market value. This is a surplus, but it has not yet been realised – i.e. the investments will have to be sold to actually realise that profit. They also have designated funds, which are part of the unrestricted funds of the charity. Note 11 to the accounts tells us that these have been designated for the purchase of new equipment for the cafe. This is like a charity saving up for items it plans to buy or projects it wishes to fund. The charity is not obliged to spend the funds on that particular purpose; legally it must spend its funds to further the charitable objects, but there is no further restriction and the trustees could later decide to re-designate the funds to something of higher priority.

7. They receive most of their income from statutory grants and contracts from local government. These are for the three main areas of work: £70,000 for advice and information; £80,000 for outreach work and £95,000 for the cafe training project. They also earn some income from the cafe.

8. They are dependent on statutory sources for most of their income, even though this comes in three different tranches. They might be able to increase the earned income from the cafe, but this would not be significant.

9. They spend a very high proportion of their income on staff costs. These amount to £211,329 out of income of £271,665, which is nearly 78%.

10. They spend a tiny proportion of income on fundraising and publicity: just £2,562 or 0.9%. They spend a little more on management and administration of the charity: £10,077 or 3.7%.

General comment

This is a fairly small charity running services with statutory funding. It is vulnerable to changes in the political climate, or economic changes affecting local government funding, and this would directly affect staffing levels and services. Most of its activity is concentrated on service provision and little time or money is apparently spent on fundraising or general administration. It has a few fixed assets, but owns little property. It has a small 'buffer' in terms of some general funds which are held partly as and investment in unit trusts and partly in cash.

Chapter 8

COMPUTERISATION

People who do not like writing up their accounting records often think that a computer will be the answer. In my view, this is the last thing they should consider! It is wiser to set up a good manual system first and then consider computerised options. Computers can certainly assist in the financial management of an organisation, but they can also hinder it. Proper use of computers should be carefully planned and should be part of an organisation-wide information technology strategy.

This chapter does not attempt to be a specialist guide on the whole strategy an organisation should adopt for the use of computers. It does attempt to clarify some points on the use of computers in financial management and to help you think through the decisions your own organisation may face. A book cannot tell you which computer software package to buy and this chapter does not attempt to be a purchaser's guide. You really need to make an assessment of your needs first and then look at the options available at the time. New products are coming onto the market all the time and you may need advice from someone who is independent and knowledgeable about the market.

Software

Software is the programs which run on a computer; the computer itself is the hardware. The most important decisions you make will be about the type of software you need and this should be considered first. The hardware decision will follow logically, as you will know the type of equipment you need after you have assessed your software needs. Software can be designed for the particular needs of your organisation (bespoke software), but this is usually beyond the budget (or needs) of most smaller organisations. It also carries far more risk and software packages may be purchased off the shelf for most tasks. The main types of software for most office and finance functions are:

◆ word-processing
◆ database
◆ spreadsheet
◆ accounting package
◆ payroll package.

Word-processing

Writing letters and reports will usually be the main use of computers in an office. You may wish to consider using word-processing software that will allow you to integrate figures from another package for a finance report. You will also be able to use a word-processing package to send out a standard letter to members or donors by using the mail merge function.

Many word-processing packages will also allow you to do a certain amount of design and so they can be used for writing newsletters and publications. However, if you are serious about designing written material, then you would need a desktop publishing package.

Things to consider when buying an off-the-shelf package

◆ Will it do the job?

◆ Will it integrate into other systems?

◆ Can we get software maintenance and support and what will it cost?

◆ Have we got enough space on our computer(s)?

◆ Can we add bolt-on software for our own specialist use?

Database

Membership charities and charities doing a large amount of fundraising from individuals will usually already have database packages for holding this information. You can buy a basic package, which is like an empty card index system – you buy the box and the cards and then set the system up. You can design the layout of the cards and reports which will access and sort the information held on the database. A database will need careful thought as to how you will want to use the information and it will probably take some time to enter all the information onto it. Once set up, however, it can become one of the most powerful and valuable parts of your organisation. You will be able to use it to send letters direct from the system or in conjunction with a word-processing package.

A database of members will usually contain details of when members paid their subscription. It therefore contains financial information and may form part of the accounting records. It is wise to try and set up systems in such a way that this information does not have to be duplicated for the financial records. There may be difficulties if the financial year and the subscription year are different, or in other ways if a clear cut-off point is not operated on the membership database. A membership database that only records that the subscription was paid, with no further details, would be insufficient as a financial record. The date and amount of the receipt is needed, and probably the date banked and a reference such as the paying in slip number or bank statement number if paid direct into the bank account. The membership database could then be used to produce a list of membership receipts in detail and the same level of detail would not be needed in the cash book. The database will also be useful to the auditors when testing membership income.

In a similar way, a database of donors may be set up to keep records of requests for funding and the responses. Again this can be done in such a way that the record of receipts provides further detail beyond the cash book. It will also be useful to the auditors when testing income.

Organisations providing services may wish to use a database as a log of those using services and then as a mailing list. The database could also be set up to produce invoices if you charge for goods or services. Entering the date of payment and the amount received would mean that the database could then also be a sales ledger. This information would need to be duplicated in the main accounts, although only the totals would have to be input.

These suggestions are just examples of ways in which you might explore the best use of systems and computer options. A database can be a part of the wider accounting records.

Fundraising Packages

Specialist database packages can be bought which handle all the record keeping for managing a fundraising department. Many will be designed specifically to manage gift aid administration and have already designed the cards and the reports for you to deal with gift aid donations. This cuts down the amount of time-consuming administration normally associated with tax recovery on gift aid. However, you need to check that the system has been set up in the way you need it. For example, you may have donors who give by monthly standing order. If the system is only geared up to handle annual donations, it will not be suitable for your organisation. You may also want a package that can handle other donations, such as payroll giving, so check this also. Some packages come with integrated accounting software, so you need to appraise this part of the software in case it is not suitable for your organisation.

Spreadsheet

Spreadsheet packages are a computerised form of a large sheet of paper with a grid format on it. The great advantage with a spreadsheet is that it can perform calculations for you. It is also very easy to learn and start using a spreadsheet package. It is ideal for:
- budget preparation
- budget reports (e.g. comparing budget to actual)
- cash flow forecasts
- designing some forms
- summarising figures from main cash books
- writing financial reports (sections with calculations).

It will allow you to make amendments and will automatically recalculate the totals. Thus you can set up a cashflow forecast at the beginning of the year, for example, and then amend it as you obtain better information. You can enter the actual figures in as these become known or you can delete the months that have passed and add on new months at the end.

Some people use spreadsheets for writing up cash books instead of a manual cash book. This is an option, but the following points should be considered:

◆ it is easy to delete figures by mistake
◆ it is easy to put figures in the wrong column or row
◆ it is easy to assume that a formula is still correctly set up when in fact it is wrong because you have changed something else
◆ a mistake in setting it up will make the whole thing wrong
◆ it can be difficult for other people to access
◆ if it is a large spreadsheet it can be difficult to read when you print it out (you have to glue pieces of paper together and it is still difficult to scan across it all)
◆ you need to ensure that cross checks are built in to ensure that your spreadsheet adds across as well as down.

In general, it is just as easy to keep a manual cash book if the number of transactions is small. Total each month in the cash book and then use the spreadsheet to add up the months. If the number of transactions is large or growing, then consider using an appropriate accounting software package, which will be a better investment of your time in the long run.

Sophisticated users of spreadsheets will develop many more uses of their packages; with a little time invested you could soon be producing colour graphs for your reports. Spreadsheet packages are useful for work with statistics as well as accounts and can also sort the information.

Accounting Package

An accounting package is a whole system for the bookkeeping of the organisation. Every accounting software package will be based on the double entry bookkeeping system and so emulate a full manual bookkeeping system. You will need to have a sound understanding of double entry bookkeeping and the meaning of terms such as debit and credit. It may be wise to go on a training course to learn double entry bookkeeping and basic accounting before you attempt to computerise your accounts on an accounting software package. Trying to learn both the accounts and the computer aspects of a new system is quite daunting. In addition, you will need to make decisions about how you want the system to be set up before you can begin using your accounting software. These decisions will be difficult unless you have a clear idea of what you want out of the system and you can picture how it will work.

Accounting software packages will contain the various elements of the full bookkeeping system (see Chapter 5, p81). The nominal ledger is the central pillar of the whole system and every system will have this. The sales and purchase ledgers are often optional extras, as are management tools such as a stock control file and invoicing system.

Software varies as to whether exact equivalents of the cash book, sales day book, purchase day book and petty cash book are part of the system. Sometimes they are present as an inherent part of the system, but you do not see them as such. You will usually be able to print out reports to show the receipts, payments, purchases or sales for a particular period. You may wish to keep these reports in a folder to create your own daybook.

Once all the information has been entered, the totals on the nominal ledger accounts can be printed out in a list, known as a trial balance. This shows the amount on each account and whether the amount is a debit or a credit balance. This is the starting point for the preparation of accounts and the next step is to check certain key accounts and look into any balances which seem unusual. On most systems you will then be able to make adjusting entries, usually called journal entries. You will usually be able to produce a profit and loss account and balance sheet as the next stage.

On some systems, you will be able to amend the profit and loss account to an income and expenditure account. Few systems can produce a Statement of Financial Activities, but you should be able to get the information from the system and then transfer it to the correct format. Most systems will produce accounts, but the flexibility will vary from package to package.

Few systems are specialist charity systems; most accounting software has been written with the commercial trader in mind. This will be fine for trading subsidiaries of charities and many elements of a commercial system will still apply to charities. Every organisation needs a nominal ledger, many will need a purchase ledger. Charities selling goods or services will often need a sales ledger. These will all be the same whatever your constitution is. This means that you should not be put off by the fact that a package has been written for a commercial user; what you should look for is flexibility. You should look for a system that allows you the freedom to use the parts of the system that you do need and ignore the parts that you don't. Some packages are designed as modules so you only buy the modules you need; for example, you only buy the sales ledger module if you want to run a sales ledger.

Payroll Package

Most payroll packages are very similar and so the choice should not be too difficult. The preparation of the payroll is a standardised task and all packages will follow Inland Revenue rules and produce the records and forms required. The package should include an automatic update service for changes to the tax rates, personal allowances and so on. Check whether there is an extra charge for this service. You also need to check that the software company is well established and so able to fulfil its commitments. You would have to abandon a package that was no longer supported or updated. Many payroll packages are a module that can link into an accounting package. An integrated approach can be useful as the transfers to the nominal ledger are undertaken automatically rather than manually. You should consider the following when choosing a payroll package:

◆ If you have weekly paid staff, can the package process weekly salaries as well as monthly?

◆ Does the package produce all the end of year returns required by the Inland Revenue?

◆ Is there a facility for the preparation of Inland Revenue forms P11D (Return of Expenses and Benefits)?

◆ Can staff costs be analysed into cost centres?

◆ Can the system deal with overtime, other additional payments, or varying hours?

◆ Does the system include Statutory Sick Pay and Statutory Maternity Pay?

◆ Can other deductions be made from net pay, such as union dues or loan repayments?

When to Computerise Accounts

When should an organisation buy an accounting software package and transfer all their bookkeeping and accounting onto it? The main advantage of computerising your accounts is that it should save time overall. Initially it will take time to set up and learn the system and to enter the data onto it. Therefore the organisation should have a high enough volume of transactions to make the setting up worthwhile. Computers are good at handling a large volume of similar transactions. If your organisation only has about 20 transactions a month, then it is likely that the bookkeeping and accounting for the whole year could be done manually in the time it would take to set up a computerised package. However, you may wish to consider computerising when the volume of transactions is low if the organisation is growing. It is certainly going to be easier to learn the system and sort out teething problems whilst the organisation is small. You will need to be careful to choose a system which will be big enough for the organisation in the long run.

Charities differ from trading organisations in that the gross income or turnover of a charity might be quite small and yet the bookkeeping and accounting needs to be quite complex. This arises from the need for fund accounting under the Charity Commission's *Statement of Recommended Practice* (SORP), the requirements of funders and the variety of sources of income and number of projects a charity may have. A trader may have just one source of income – sales of goods or services – and a straightforward list of expenditure items. Charities will usually be more complex than this. In addition, their activities will often vary from year to year as new projects or activities are brought in and old ones discontinued. The complexity of charity accounting may mean that a computerised system will save the organisation a lot of time.

Someone needs to be able to set up and operate the new accounting software once it has been purchased. You must allow for the cost of staff training if you do not have someone who is already competent in the system. Computerising the accounts will be a big step for most organisations and if the people in the organisation are not happy or ready for it, it will fail. It will be more difficult for people just to look up when an invoice was paid (at first, anyway) and there may be resistance to learning about the new system.

Advantages of Computerised Accounts

◆ Standardised format
◆ Quick to enter data
◆ Manual calculations eliminated
◆ System will only allow balancing entries
◆ Reports produced from system

Disadvantages of a Computerised System

◆ Less accessible for non-financial people in organisation
◆ Personnel using the system need training
◆ Untrained personnel may make mistakes which are difficult and costly to resolve
◆ Poorly referenced systems may make the audit more difficult
◆ Cheap or inappropriate packages may not incorporate sufficient controls

---

The process of computerising accounting records has several stages:

◆ Assessing the organisation's needs
◆ Preparing a specification
◆ Choosing a package
◆ Implementation plan
◆ Testing
◆ Parallel running
◆ System operational.

Assessing the Organisation's Needs

Before you buy your software package, you need to consider the organisation's needs in terms of accounting. A focus area for such an assessment should be the recording and reporting requirements of everyone in the organisation. You need to understand what you need to get out of the system as well as what you will be putting in. You will also need to gauge the size of the system needed, access requirements and number of transactions. If possible, you should also try to think ahead to how the organisation may expand or what further information may be needed in the future.

Illustration – Charity Training Services

Charity Training Services (CTS) run short training courses in many different subjects for the voluntary and public sector. Fees are charged for the courses and most courses are led by freelance trainers. CTS itself has a small administrative staff which operates on the same premises where the courses are run.

A review of their needs reveals:

- they need a system to log bookings on courses
- they need to invoice people for course fees
- some people pay after they receive the invoice; others send payment with booking
- many customers book several courses at once for different individuals to attend training
- they have about 50 different trainers, each leading about one session per week, and submitting invoices weekly
- they only have five full-time staff
- they need a report on a weekly basis which shows the number of course bookings received and can provide details of how many people are booked onto each course
- they need a monthly report to show income and expenditure compared to budget.

The organisation decides to buy a database program that can be tailored to their needs for course management. This will be a database of customers and will also be used to produce invoices and record whether payment has been received or not. It will operate as the sales ledger of the organisation. This will be tied into the cash book receipts. They want an accounting software package that allows them to bypass the sales ledger and input receipts direct onto the nominal ledger via a cash book routine. The database will also give them the weekly reports on bookings. It will also need to provide the basic information to identify how much course income has been invoiced in advance, in order that the monthly income figures will correctly reflect the income earned for the month on courses that ran in the month.

The accounting software needs to be a simple nominal ledger system with an integrated purchase ledger. This will allow CTS to treat all their freelance trainers as suppliers and their details can be set up on the purchase ledger system. Invoices can be entered on a weekly basis and payment made on a monthly basis. Preferably the system should produce remittance advices. It may also print cheques, although the high cost of printing cheques is not acceptable to CTS at present. The staff salaries can be prepared on a manual payroll.

The nominal ledger should accept entries direct from the purchase ledger, but the sales information will have to be input by journal. A cash book module would deal with receipts and payments and the bank reconciliation. Reporting from the accounting system will be simple monthly income and expenditure (profit and loss) reports and a balance sheet. If the system can take the budget information and produce the comparisons, then fine. Otherwise, this would not be difficult to set up on a spreadsheet.

Example Questions for Needs Assessment

- How many transactions do we need to process in a month – e.g. number of purchase invoices, number of receipts and payments?
- Do we need to invoice customers for income?
- Do we sell any goods or services on credit?
- Do we only supply after cash received?
- How many different activities or areas of work do we have?
- How many different sources of income do we have?
- Is our main source of income unsolicited donations?
- How many different expenditure categories do we have in our budget?
- How many regular suppliers do we have?
- How many different cost centres?
- How are we likely to expand in the future and will this mean more cost centres?
- How many staff do we have and how do we prepare the payroll?
- What sort of reports do we want and how frequently?
- Do we need different reports for different people?

Preparing a Specification

The next stage is to write a clear specification of what the organisation wants from the system. It may not be able to get everything it wants from a package, and may have to compromise somewhere. However, it is still better to start from what you want. Each package you look at can then be measured against your specification. You can also send your specification to dealers and ask whether they can supply a package that meets most of the requirements.

It is also a good way of asking different dealers to cost out a package for you. At least you are comparing similar products.

Choosing a Package

Using the needs assessment and specification, you are now ready to go out and look at packages. Whilst there may be a great number of packages on the market, you will be able to eliminate some of them very quickly. You should then look more closely at a shortlist of two or three.

It is useful to find out from the dealer or manufacturer how many other organisations similar to your own are using the software. It is often worthwhile to take up references with existing users, as you usually find out more about the support and maintenance that way. If you can find another similar organisation using the software, ask if you can visit them. An on-site demonstration and a short conversation about how good they have found the software will give you more information than lots of brochures.

Support is very important, as things can go wrong with the system. This is increasingly important as your organisation gets larger and your computer systems more complex. You need to check that the company which should be providing the support is well established and will continue for the foreseeable future. There are numerous stories of support companies going out of business, being bought out or losing interest in the particular software you have purchased. It is not always wise to go for the cheapest option.

Look at sample reports and print outs from the system and check whether the formats will be suitable or can be easily adapted. You may be able to export the data from the accounting software to a spreadsheet package and therefore design your own reports more easily. (Check for any additional cost to do this.)

You may have to compromise on some of the points in your specification, so it is best to identify the most important points and give those priority in your selection process.

Be sure to cost in all aspects of the computerisation process before you make your choice:
♦ new hardware or upgrades
♦ software itself
♦ installation and set up
♦ software maintenance and support
♦ training.

You need to be sure that you have sufficient funds to complete the process properly – it is not sensible to buy a complex package and then find you cannot afford to train anyone to use it. You may want to compromise because of shortage of funds. If your organisation is really short of money, then think again. Is computerising the accounts the most important thing to do just now? Perhaps the money could be better spent in other ways. Avoid mistakes at the other extreme as well – there is no point in buying a package just because it is cheap. If it does not match up to the most important points on your specification then it will not be able to do the job. You will be no better off with a system such as this and in fact it could cost you dearly if the accountant/auditor has to do a lot of additional work at the end of the year.

Choosing Accounting Software – Example Questions

♦ Can we do cost centre accounting?
♦ Can it produce separate reports for different managers?
♦ Can it produce reports in different ways for different purposes?
♦ Can it produce reports for funders?
♦ Can it be adapted to produce proper charity accounts that comply with the SORP?
♦ Can it track restricted, unrestricted and endowment funds?
♦ Can the system cope with the size of our organisation and the complexity of our accounts?

Implementation plan

A timetable needs to be carefully thought through and agreed with members of the organisation and possibly outside people as well. The changeover to a new system may cause some disruption to payments, for example, so good communication is vital to ensure that you do not lose the goodwill of suppliers. You do not want everyone to blame the new system for everything, especially when it is really due to lack of human planning. You need to think about the work needed to install a new system and the time required. Make room in your plan for things to wrong, so that you can catch up and overall be on time with the whole implementation.

Illustration – Charity Training Services

CTS has chosen the software it wishes to use. It has now identified the following tasks which need to be undertaken to implement the new system. The list is not in any particular order.

◆ Check names and addresses of existing customers.

◆ Transfer existing customer details onto new database.

◆ Set up records in database with necessary fields.

◆ Write up existing manual cash book up to date.

◆ Perform bank reconciliation up to date.

◆ Prepare list of outstanding amounts due from customers and reconcile to a sales ledger control account.

◆ Put details of courses onto database.

◆ Put details of tutors and suppliers onto purchase ledger.

◆ Set up nominal ledger accounts.

◆ Enter test transactions and check output.

◆ Set up reports required from database.

◆ Set up reports required from accounting software.

◆ Enter opening balances onto nominal ledger.

◆ Inform trainers and other suppliers of change to new system.

◆ Obtain banking details from trainers and suppliers so that payments can be made direct.

◆ Internal memo to explain implementation.

◆ Training sessions for finance staff.

◆ Training sessions for others.

The next task for CTS would be to check for completeness, then to organise this list into a timetable. If there are several staff involved, then several tasks can be undertaken concurrently. This is best worked out using a chart to plan the tasks, the timing and who should be doing it. If there are several people involved, then they need to work as a team and a team leader should be in charge of the overall implementation. Team meetings will help to ensure that things go according to plan. If they are using consultants, it is important that they agree the implementation plan and timetable with them. They will then need regular meetings to monitor the plan.

(Note that many of the tasks on the list are not just about the new system; it is essential that your accounting records are up to date, balanced, checked and accurate before you put them onto the new system.)

Testing

When you get your new software, it is tempting to switch on and start using it straight away. Even after some training, however, you will still have a lot to learn about the new system and how you will be able to use it for your own organisation. It is much better, therefore, to set up a dummy organisation and enter some test data. If you have a system that will allow you to set up several companies, then set one up just for training and testing. Otherwise, check that you can install the software twice or ask your dealer for help. The best test will be to set up some real records and process some real transactions from a past month. This will help you to sort out how you want to reference transactions on the computer, and what paperwork you will need to keep. How will you file paperwork? How will you mark it to show that it has been entered? How do you ensure that transactions do not get entered twice or missed? How will you check that the computer record is accurate?

Testing is an important part of the whole implementation. Even on well established accounting software packages, where you do not need to test the software as such, you need to test the operation for your own organisation. It is also a good opportunity to familiarise yourself with the package. All packages have little idiosyncrasies and it is better to find these out on test data, rather than waste a lot of work on real data. Only when you are satisfied that the tests are satisfactory should you progress on to the next stage.

Parallel running

Most implementation plans will allow a period of parallel running of the old system alongside the new system. This is extra work, but does allow the opportunity to check the accuracy of the new system. It also means that the old system can still be used for management information whilst the implementation of the new system is underway.

Usually a parallel run will mean that the transactions for a week or a month are entered onto the old system and then onto the new system as well. The results are then compared to ensure that the results on the new system are complete and accurate.

It is not obligatory to parallel run and it may not be very useful if the two systems are completely different. Alternatively, you should take time to check in some detail that the transactions have been correctly processed.

System operational

Having trained everyone, tested and parallel run everything, you should be ready for the systems to be fully operational. It is useful to write your own operations manual as you go along. Although the software will have its own manual, you may need to write something very simple for people in the organisation who only need to access information occasionally. This will also be useful for new staff. An operations manual will also include your own procedures and checks, not simply the computer based functions. So, for example, the procedure for processing a purchase invoice from a supplier can include matching to the purchase order, checks for arithmetical accuracy and approval by the appropriate person.

Having established a system, it will need to be kept under review and developed as new demands are made on it.

Pitfalls to Avoid

Computerising your accounts can save a lot of time and money; on the other hand, it can lead to expensive mistakes. Some of the pitfalls to avoid are:

◆ don't skimp on training – good systems are usually under-utilised and so the real benefits are missed because staff do not know how to use the system properly or to its full extent;

◆ don't skimp on software – a cheap but inappropriate package will be a waste of money, not a cost saving. Don't just buy for today, think ahead and buy for tomorrow;

◆ don't rush into setting up a system – you need to think through the whole operation and plan carefully. You do not have to start your new system at the beginning of the financial year; it is not a problem to transfer the balances onto the new nominal ledger and it is better to have prepared for the changeover properly, than to get in a mess trying to rush for implementation at the beginning of a new financial year;

◆ don't underestimate the amount of time and effort a new system will require – it will take time for the benefits to be reaped;

◆ don't forget to set up appropriate controls and checks as part of the system. You still need to perform reconciliations on key control accounts and to check reports;

◆ don't forget to set up good paper based systems for controlling what goes into the computer. You will need to batch documents, set up checks to ensure they are entered once only and set up good filing systems;

◆ don't forget to set up a sensible referencing system so that transactions can be traced from one part of the system to another. This must include the paper records as well as the computer records;

◆ don't make adjustments to the accounting records without recording the reason for the entry. A system of numbered journal vouchers or forms to show the entry, the reason for it, the date, and the person making the entry is needed. Journal entries should also be authorised where there are several people in the department;

♦ don't forget to make back-ups of the information you have on the system on a regular basis.

Other Considerations

Cost Centre Accounting

Most charities will have different activities or projects and will need to keep track of the costs of individual projects. With the SORP on charity accounting, there will also be a need to identify restricted funds and to keep track of expenditure on those individual funds. Additionally, many funders require reports on how their funds have been spent. This can lead to complicated accounting and reporting requirements for even quite small charities.

An accounting package needs to keep records in a way that runs parallel to your budget. This will usually involve a cost centre approach for incoming and outgoing resources. The nominal ledger will have to be designed so that the traditional income and expenditure accounts are there, such as salaries, rent, rates, insurance and so on. In addition, the analysis should identify the project, activity, or department that the income or expenditure item belongs to, such as marketing, fundraising, education. These are the cost centres. Usually the coding system of the nominal ledger will allow you to code all the entries for the same cost centre with the same prefix or suffix. In a similar way all the entries for a particular account, say telephone, will have the same code. The nominal ledger can then sort the information either by cost centre, or by account or both. So you can have a report showing all the balances relating to a particular cost centre to give you information on a project's income and expenditure. You can also have a trial balance that shows the totals for all accounts without analysing into cost centres to give you the organisational income and expenditure account. You may also be able to get further reports depending on the system. For preparation of accounts under the SORP, the cost centre report and the trial balance as described above are essential.

Some systems go further and can accommodate another analysis code. This may allow you to identify restricted and unrestricted funds. For some organisations, this may be essential if projects have funding from several sources, not all of which are restricted. Three-way analysis can be used in a number of ways in large organisations. Other systems allow you total flexibility in the nominal ledger structure and the cost centre accounting is simply a part of the list of accounts. For reports to be produced in the way in which you want, you have to build up the coding of the nominal ledger in the right way.

Cost centre accounting is likely to be essential for nearly all large charities. Obviously, for smaller charities with fewer projects, this may not be such a difficult issue. For larger charities with different sites, branches, projects and activities, it will be a major part of the planning exercise to design the nominal ledger structure, coding and reporting.

Accounting for VAT

For charities that are not registered for VAT, this will present no problems. Although the accounting software will allow you to analyse out the VAT, you ignore this and enter all expenditure inclusive of VAT.

For charities that are registered for VAT, the VAT on all expenditure should be analysed out when entered. Most charities are only partially exempt for VAT purposes and so not all the VAT on purchases (input VAT) will be recoverable. Input VAT has to be identified to the different categories of VAT according to the activity to which the purchase relates. (See Chapter 10 for VAT glossary and explanations of terms.) You need to keep several codes or accounts for input VAT as follows:

- ◆ input VAT on purchases directly related to non-business activity
- ◆ input VAT on purchases directly related to exempt activity
- ◆ input VAT on purchases directly related to taxable activity
- ◆ input VAT on purchases not directly related to a particular activity (non-attributable).

This will enable you to extract the information you need for the preparation of the VAT return without too much further calculation. You will need to check whether the organisation is below the *de minimis* limit for partial exemption and calculate the proportion of the non-attributable VAT that may be recovered. The VAT account(s) should then be cleared down after the VAT return has been prepared. The amount recoverable or payable can be on the VAT control account, but the irrecoverable VAT should be transferred to an expenditure account (written off). Usually a separate account called Irrecoverable VAT is set up for this.

Security

It is important that accounting records and other information is safe from corruption and accessible only to those authorised to read it. Each user should have a password, which they have to type in before they can get into the system. You will be able to set up your system so that some areas are 'read only' to certain users. They may also be denied access entirely to certain areas, so that sensitive information, such as salary details, is accessible only to certain people. This system of passwords can also be used to ensure that only trained personnel are entering information onto the system or altering records. This would prevent anyone other than the payroll officer changing the salary rates, for example.

The system also needs to be protected from corruption by computer viruses. If you operate a stand alone personal computer or a small network without modem links, you can prevent viruses entering the system by prohibiting anyone from installing any of their own software onto the system. Staff should not be allowed to bring in their own programs (or games!). Larger networks and computers using E-mail or the Internet should have virus-detecting software installed and run regularly.

Back-ups

You will need to consider how you will back-up information on the computer. You should think about what would happen in the event of computer disks corrupting or of a fire or theft. (Remember, thieves are targeting the hard disk in your computer and leaving the rest behind, so you would lose the essential part of your computer.)

Firstly, you should keep a back-up of the original disks containing the software in a safe place – either in a fire safe or on other premises. These may also be needed in the event of a hard disk failure.

Next you need to consider how you will keep regular back-ups of the data. If there is a large volume of information and daily entries are made, then a back-up should be made at the end of every day. If you are a smaller user, then you may consider a weekly back-up is sufficient, but remember, if anything happens you are going to lose everything since your last back-up. It will be very time-consuming if you have to enter a lot of data again.

Most computer users operate a 'grandfather, father, son' system. This means that you have three sets of back-up disks or tapes. At the end of day one, you use set A. At the end of day two, you use set B (leaving set A intact). At the end of day three, you use set C. At the end of day four you use set A again, overwriting the previous back-up. You then continue in this cyclical fashion. The idea behind this is that you have at least three chances of a good back-up. If data does become corrupted, it is possible that you would not notice immediately. So you could do your back-up on set C, but this would have the corrupted data on it. You would then need to go back to set B or set A – hopefully, you would find uncorrupted data.

For accounting systems, it is usual to keep a permanent back-up for a complete year's transactions or some other convenient period.

Summary

Computerised systems can certainly help your organisation to manage administration and finance more effectively. To achieve this, the systems have to be properly planned and implemented. You also have to have adequate funds to install and maintain all the systems, as well as train staff to a sufficient standard.

SECTION 3

TAX AND VAT

Chapter 9

TAX AND TRADING

One of the main advantages of charitable status is the tax relief that is available. Charities are exempt from income tax, corporation tax and capital gains tax on all income applied for charitable purposes. Additionally, charities do not pay stamp duty on transactions such as the purchase of property. Charities also receive 80% relief on business rates for the premises they occupy, which may be extended to 100% relief at the discretion of the local authority. Charities may also reclaim tax on gifts (covered in more detail in Chapter 11) and obtain some relief from VAT (covered in more detail in Chapter 10).

These tax reliefs will be forfeited if a charity is in breach of the special conditions attached to them. Certainly charities which trade will need to consider how they should structure their activities to avoid loss of valuable tax reliefs and to minimise the cost of tax on potentially taxable activities. Charities must also consider the legal implications of straying too far into trading, as this may mean that the trustees are acting in breach of the charity's governing instrument. We will first look at the legal position of charities in relation to trading.

CHARITY TRADING AND THE LAW

A charity must act in accordance with its constitution, so trading which is undertaken in the course of carrying out the main objective of the charity is quite legitimate. There can be a problem with fundraising which is trading, such as the sale of Christmas cards, because the charity may have to buy the cards in order to sell them. The purchase of the cards is not likely to be an application of funds to the main charitable objects. Although the reason for the fundraising activity may be to generate funds for the main charitable purpose, this is too remote. The charity is undertaking commercial trading activities which are not permitted under charity law. Charitable trading will include the activities of charities which charge a fee for a service, such as nursing homes and independent schools, as well as the sale of goods produced by the beneficiaries of a charity. Non-charitable trading will often take the form of activities undertaken for fundraising purposes, such as regular events and the sale of goods or services. Charitable trading can be undertaken as long as it is within the charity's objects. Substantial non-charitable trading may have to be channelled through another organisation, such as a trading subsidiary.

Charities are allowed to carry on ancillary trading. Examples of this include selling refreshments to visitors at an art gallery or providing childcare facilities to people attending a training course, both of which are services ancillary to the main event.

Infrequent fundraising events with a clear fundraising purpose will not be trading, nor will traditional forms of fundraising such as public collections, flag days and such like. The sale of donated goods (in charity shops and at functions, jumble sales etc.) is not treated as trading, but seen as the conversion of donations into cash. Small scale non-charitable trading will also be ignored, where this is insignificant compared to the charitable trading activities and in absolute amounts. The legal view on what is small-scale trading has been aligned with the Inland Revenue guidance on this aspect and is therefore examined in more detail below.

CHARITY TRADING AND TAX

Charities are exempt from paying corporation tax, income tax and capital gains tax providing the income is applied for charitable purposes. (The main legislation giving the exemption is contained in Section 505 of the Income and Corporation Taxes Act 1988.) The Inland Revenue will ask to see the accounts of charities periodically to check that the income is being applied for charitable purposes. In addition, the Inland Revenue may ask charities to complete a corporation tax return (form CT600). Note that a penalty of £100 may be charged if a company fails to make a return if requested, or sends it in late (a company has 12 months after the financial year end in which to file the return).

The exemption is extended to trading profits used for charitable purposes providing:

◆ the trade is carrying out the primary purpose of the charity, OR
◆ the trade is undertaken by the beneficiaries of the charity.

For example, the sale of publications about the cause espoused by the charity, or fees for residential care, would constitute primary purpose trading.

There are also no problems with investment income, interest received and rent received; the Inland Revenue treats such income as income derived from the charity's assets, but not trading as such, so it is exempt from tax under a clause in the relevant legislation. A similar situation has been established for the sale of donated goods, seen as the conversion of goods into cash but still the receipt of a donation. The implications for VAT are slightly different and care must be taken as the VAT rules for business activities are not the same as the tax rules on trading activities. Many charities will be registered for VAT and undertaking business activities on which it has to charge VAT. No charity should be paying income tax or corporation tax.

Definition of Trading

Trading is not very clearly defined in the legislation; however, numerous cases have been to court over the question of whether a trade exists or not and so a body of case law has been built up. The main points the Inland Revenue looks for are:

◆ Repetition – where the trading is regular rather than a one-off event
◆ Profit motive – generally the profit motive should be present for trading to exist, even though a profit is not always actually made
◆ Mechanism for selling – the existence of a shop, catalogue or other means for the sale of the goods or services indicates the existence of a trade
◆ Acquisition of items for re-sale – buying goods with the intention of reselling them rather than consuming them will indicate a trade.

The Inland Revenue could decide that a trade is being undertaken even if only one of the above criteria is fulfilled. It is unwise to rely on your own interpretation of the facts to decide that your organisation is not trading and therefore will not be liable to tax.

Small-scale Trading Exemption

Since April 2000, a new exemption has been introduced allowing trading activities within charities up to specified limits:

◆ Trading activity will be exempt from tax if turnover from that activity is less than £5,000 in the year.
◆ Trading activity will also be exempt if the turnover from the trade is less than 25% of the gross income of the charity, or less than £50,000, whichever is the lower.

This means that charities with a small operation selling Christmas cards or similar activities will be allowed to undertake the activities through the charity.

Fundraising Activities

As an extra statutory concession, the Inland Revenue allows charities to undertake small fundraising activities without incurring tax liabilities. The types of activities they list as examples are 'bazaars, jumble sales, gymkhanas, carnivals, firework displays'. In practice, the exemption will be extended to all small-scale fundraising events providing:

◆ The charity is not regularly carrying out these trading activities.
◆ The trading is not in competition with other traders.
◆ The activities are supported substantially because the public is aware that any profits will be donated to charity.
◆ The profits are applied for charitable purposes.

From April 2000, there are new rules which extend the tax exemption for fundraising activities. These are now matched to the rules for VAT. Fundraising events no longer have to be one-off – charities may have 15 events of the same kind in the same location in one financial year. Events may be held by the charity or its trading subsidiary, but the limit of 15 would apply to them jointly.

Events can be widely interpreted, so that it can include an event on the internet and it does include participatory events such as golf days.

Events do have to be organised with a clear fundraising purpose, which should be made known to the public. Any events which create a distortion of competition and place a commercial enterprise at a disadvantage will not be exempt fundraising events.

Small-scale events can be ignored, as long as the aggregate gross takings from events of that type in that location do not exceed £1,000 in a week. This means that jumble sales and coffee mornings are not included when counting up the number of events.

Mutual Trading

Mutual trading is a situation in which members of a group contribute to the costs of an activity. Although surpluses may be created, the surplus is not taxable if it can, by the rules of the organisation, only be reinvested in the activity or repaid to the contributors. Charities cannot undertake mutual trading because the definition of mutual trading requires that there is a defined group of people who contribute and benefit from the activities. Since there is no public benefit, such an organisation would not be registered as a charity in the first place. However, certain community groups and cooperative ventures denied charitable status may be able to claim that their activities amount to mutual trading and thereby avoid large tax bills.

Non-Charitable Voluntary Organisations

Some organisations, such as campaigning groups, are ineligible for charitable status, even though they operate in a similar way to charities and do not distribute profits. Because they do not have charitable status these organisations do not qualify for tax exemptions and may find that they have to pay tax on any surplus at the end of the financial year. However, if the majority of their income is from voluntary sources, then the Inland Revenue will not usually seek to tax it. Additionally, if they do have some trading activity, such as the sale of publications, then it is possible to prepare a separate tax computation for that activity. This should bring in the direct costs and a proportion of the overheads to arrive at the taxable profit figure. The taxable profit is often very low and so the tax payable not significant. The organisation will, however, have to pay tax on interest earned and no exemption from this is available for non-charitable voluntary organisations.

Trading Subsidiaries

The common way to deal with trading which does not fall within the exemptions (i.e. non-charitable trading) is to channel the income and expenditure relating to those activities through a separate company. Usually the company will be an ordinary share company, with general trading objects and the usual clauses for a commercial undertaking. It is normal for two shares to be issued which are usually owned by the charity, or by charity trustees who hold them on trust for the benefit of the charity. Either way, the charity should control the trading company and decide who the director/s will be, thus making the company a subsidiary of the charity.

A company must have a minimum of one director, but there will usually be several. It is tempting to make all the trustees of the charity the directors of the trading company, however, this is unwise and the Charity Commission advise against it. If the two boards are exactly the same, then there could be a conflict of interest. The charity trustees must always have regard to the interests of the beneficiaries of the charity and so must protect its assets and minimise risk. Whilst the trading subsidiary may wish to maximise profits for the benefit of the charity, there may be occasions where a conflict could arise, such as agreeing a management charge (that is, a payment made by the company for the services – staff time, for example – of the charity) between the two organisations.

Advantages of a Separate Trading Subsidiary	Disadvantages of a Separate Trading Subsidiary
◆ Protects charity from tax liability	◆ A more complex structure with added costs – incorporation, audit, professional advice
◆ Clarifies objectives for each part of organisation	◆ Knowledge of very specific tax rules needed
◆ Limited liability status for separate trading company may protect charitable funds in the event of a mistake	◆ Company must operate at 'arm's length' to the charity
◆ Allows you to undertake certain activities which a registered charity may not	◆ There may have to be management charges between company and charity
◆ May be convenient for VAT planning	◆ Rate relief may be lost

Many charities like to have some representation on the board of directors of the trading company, to ensure that they exercise control in practice as well as in theory. This could be one or two employees of the charity and one or two trustees. Preferably they should be people with business experience. It may also be appropriate to have one or two senior employees of the trading company on the board of directors, as one might in a commercial setting. It is worth remembering that the board of directors of a trading company does not have to be large. It is not the same as the board of trustees of a charity, where you may be trying to represent various different interests.

The charity will need to review how the subsidiary is managed, once it is established. The AGM of the trading subsidiary is an opportunity for the charity to receive a proper report of the activities of the subsidiary over the past year and its plans for the next. The charity can ensure that the strategic objectives of the company are not in conflict with its own and that the return is satisfactory. This is part of the trustees' governance role and in keeping with their duty to monitor the charity's investments.

One of the benefits of channelling trading activities through a separate company is that a certain clarity of objectives is achieved. The main objective of a trading company is fundraising for the charity and it should be trying to maximise profits and the return on capital. It can therefore be measured by fairly standard commercial criteria. It is true that a certain amount of image enhancement or public profile may be achieved as well, but this should not be used to justify loss-making trading activities. A charity is more likely to prop up a loss making activity if it is kept under the charity umbrella, whereas this becomes harder to justify once the activity is hived off into a separate trading company.

Profit Shedding

In order for the arrangement to work, the trading company must shed its taxable profits by tax-effective transfer to the charity. This is usually achieved by gift aid.

The trading subsidiary can make the gift aid payment to the charity up to nine months after the end of the company's financial year. The gift aid may be included in the trading subsidiary's corporation tax computation for the financial year. This gives the company time to draw up accounts and calculate the taxable profit.

The trading subsidiary can also make transfers at various points during the year by gift aid, and then just make a final payment after the end of the financial year to mop up the rest of the profit. This use of gift aid works in the same way as for any company and no forms or declarations are required. The amount paid to the charity is the gross amount and the charity does not claim back any tax. The trading subsidiary only has to enter the gift aid payment on its corporation tax return.

Financing the Trading

Whatever the activity, the charity needs to consider how the activity will be financed. Working capital may be needed for stock, premises or equipment and therefore charitable funds may be needed to finance the initial start up costs.

Investment Powers

If the charity uses its own funds to finance the initial working capital of the trading subsidiary this amounts to an investment by the charity, and the rules on such an investment apply just as for any other investment. The charity must have the power to invest as part of its constitution. Note that if the charity does not have the appropriate power to invest, then it may not even buy a trading company, spend funds on setting one up or spend just £2 on the minimum of shares. If this is the case, then the charity should amend its constitution and agree the amendment with the Charity Commission. The power to invest must be sorted out before the charity embarks on trading activities. (See Chapter 4 Investment, for more details.)

Commercial Loan

Assuming the charity has investment powers, the trustees must give careful consideration to the decision to invest and the most appropriate way to fund the working capital. One option is to seek a commercial loan from a bank or similar lender. Commercial lenders will be reluctant to lend to a company which is really just a 'shell' – which is what the trading subsidiary of a charity will be – and because the company will be transferring all its profits to the charity, it will never have a very healthy balance sheet. It is also likely to have few assets, so the security for a commercial lender will be scant. It is therefore likely that the lender would seek guarantees from the charity. This presents difficulties for charities because trustees would probably be in breach of trust if a guarantee was called upon and the charity's assets were lost to satisfy the liabilities of the trading company. In addition, a commercial loan is an expensive way of funding the trading, since the company will be paying interest to a third party instead of paying it to the charity. If the charity has the spare funds to invest in the trading company, a commercial loan would be a wasteful course of action.

It may be possible to obtain cheaper loan finance from one of the sources being established to lend to charities. Often, the terms are not as onerous as normal commercial loans and the lenders may lend without the security of fixed assets. (See Further Information.)

Loan from the Charity

The most common route for funding the working capital of the trading company is for the charity to lend it the money. This should be properly assessed, just as if the loan were to an external body. The trustees should receive appropriate documents, such as a business plan, to satisfy themselves that the trading activity is viable. The trustees' decision should be taken at a trustees' meeting and minuted. There should be a loan agreement and commercial rates of interest should be charged. The interest should be actually paid over; it is not sufficient for an entry simply to be made in the accounting records. There should be a charge over the trading company's assets, including stock, debtors and cash balances (it is usual to take a fixed and floating charge). This has to be registered at Companies House and means that the charity has the power to appoint a receiver and has first call on the assets of the company should it become insolvent.

Charity Loans to Subsidiary Trading Companies

Remember the following key points when considering a loan to a trading company:

◆ Assess the loan request as if it were from an external body

◆ Document the decision

◆ Ensure that a business plan is drawn up

◆ Execute a loan agreement

◆ The trading company should pay a commercial rate of interest to the charity

◆ The charity should have charge over the trading company's assets.

Shares

The charity could buy more than the minimum number of shares in the trading company. This would then provide the company with some or all of the capital needed to start up. The decision to buy share capital would have to be made as any other investment decision. The disadvantage with investment by shares is that the charity will have few ways of ever recouping its investment. The shareholders are the last to be paid out in the event of a winding up and the share capital cannot easily be repaid if the company continues trading. It is possible for the company to buy its own shares back, although this is unlikely to be possible in the situation where the profits are being passed up to the charity. The charity might be able to sell the company to a commercial purchaser at some point, but this is also an unlikely route. Hence, share capital more or less permanently ties up the charity's money, whereas there is the possibility that a loan will be repaid. Having said all that, this may well be the appropriate course of action for a trading company that wished to have a 'clean break' from the parent charity.

Retaining profits

A trading company could retain profits so that it was able to fund its own working capital requirements.

Since 1 April 2002, corporation tax is zero on profits up to £10,000 in a financial year. Charity trading subsidiaries can use the zero-rate tax band to retain some profits without incurring tax liabilities. Over a number of years, this may be built up into a sufficient reserve to fund the working capital.

Shared Premises, Facilities or Staffing

If the trading company uses any facilities or staff time paid for by the charity, then a service charge or management charge must be made. The charity should charge these facilities at cost and will have to bear in mind that these will be subject to VAT if the charity exceeds the VAT threshold. Care must be taken that the principal of the subsidiary company operating at 'arm's length' is maintained. Neither should the charity make a profit on the management services, unless they are primary purpose trading, as otherwise the profits may be taxable.

Equipment and Buildings

It is usually wiser for the charity to own the major fixed assets and then lease these to the trading subsidiary, otherwise the charity would have to lend money to the trading company and take a fixed charge over the assets. It is therefore easier for the charity to retain ownership of all significant assets (certainly property) so that it is not risking those assets. However, the VAT position will also have to be considered, in order that VAT recovery may be maximised.

Setting up a Trading Company

Before you set up a trading company, ask yourselves the following questions:

1. Do we need a trading company? Is our trading actually fulfilling the primary purpose of the charity or otherwise exempt from tax as small-scale trading, fundraising or fundraising events?
2. Does our constitution allow us to invest in the shares in of another company'?
3. Which activities should be channelled through the trading company?
4. Do those activities make a profit? What would be the working capital needs of a trading company?
5. Can the charity afford to lend or invest the working capital or will the company have to go to a commercial lender?
6. Should some of the investment be share capital?
7. What will be the charity's return on the investment and is this adequate?

8. Will the company use facilities or staff time which the charity should charge for?
9. How will the VAT position be affected?

Having decided to go ahead, you need to:

1. Buy a share company with general trading objects. Company formation agents (look in Yellow Pages) have ready-formed companies which you can buy off the shelf. You need to allow about £300, and to change the company name.
2. Decide on the amount of the charity's investment and whether this should be in the form of share capital, and allot shares accordingly.
3. Appoint directors of the company.
4. Inject some working capital and formalise any loans through proper loan agreements.
5. Ensure there are proper agreements if there are any arrangements for use of facilities, equipment and so on.
6. Set up systems to monitor profitability and liquidity.

Monitoring the Profitability of the Trading Activity

It is important that trusts monitor the effectiveness of trading subsidiaries carefully. Because the main purpose of the company is to generate profits for the trust, commercial measures may be used to judge the company's performance.

Profitability should be measured against expectations. It can also be useful to compare your performance to that of other similar operations. However, it is often difficult to get sufficient data of this sort as the information can be commercially sensitive. More usually, you monitor the trends in performance by using certain ratios (see Chapter 2, p46) and comparisons to previous years or budget. The ratios which may be useful are:

◆ return on capital employed
◆ gross profit percentage
◆ stock turnover
◆ age of debtors
◆ creditor payment period.

Other measures used in the retail trade include:
◆ turnover per staff member
◆ turnover per square foot of retail space.

Trading or Fundraising?

Having set up a trading company, there will need to be clear rules about which activities are channelled through the trading company and which activities are carried out through the charity. Charitable trading may go through the charity, as may many fundraising activities, such as exempt events and lotteries. It is advantageous for shops selling donated goods to be kept within the charity, as then the charity retains eligibility to mandatory rates relief. However, shops selling a significant proportion of new and bought-in goods will have to check the small-scale trading exemption and may need to channel activities through the trading company.

As well as considering the legal and tax issues, charities should consider how the arrangements will be managed. It may be simpler to undertake all of one type of fundraising activity, such as events, through the trading subsidiary. There is no loss or additional cost to the charity, as profits may be transferred by gift aid at regular intervals to the charity.

Sponsorship

Incoming funds which buy the funder some promotion or advertising is trading and should go through the trading company if it is significant. However sponsorship of exempt fundraising events will be considered part of the income of the fundraising event and therefore covered by the exemption.

VAT

Some activities, such as education or training and welfare, are exempt from VAT if they are undertaken by a charity. This may make a big difference when deciding which entity should undertake the activity, as the organisation may be better off if this activity is undertaken in the trading subsidiary and the VAT recovered. There will be other important VAT considerations, which will vary depending on the nature of the organisation's activities. The mix of activities will be important too, as the best arrangement for VAT purposes will have to take the rules on VAT recovery into account (see Chapter 10).

Affinity Cards

Many charities now receive funds from finance companies and banks by letting the bank use the charity's name on a credit card. These are known as affinity cards. The arrangement usually allows the bank to send publicity material about the affinity card to the charity's membership or list of supporters, in return for which the charity receives a one-off fee for every new person who signs up to the affinity card. In addition, the charity receives a commission calculated as a percentage of the purchases made by customers using the affinity card. The charity is in effect selling its mailing list and the use of its name or logo for promotional purposes to the bank or finance company. This is non-charitable trading and, if it exceeds the small-scale trading limits, should be channelled through the trading company, for which there must be an agreement between the bank and the trading company. However, the charity is the body with the name and the logo, and therefore there has to be an agreement for the bank or finance company to use to the charity's name (usually called a licence).

The first agreement should identify the promotional services being 'sold' (such as providing the mailing list) and the fee for this service. The fee will be subject to VAT at the standard rate. Customs and Excise have agreed in principle that there may then be further amounts received as donations, which are therefore outside the scope of VAT. The amount of the fee for the promotional services must be reasonable for the service provided. As a guide, Customs and Excise have stated that they would expect at least 20% of the one-off payment for new cards issued to be the VATable amount. The entire amount of commission received on the purchases made using the card is treated as a donation and is non-VATable. It would therefore be appropriate for these payments to be made direct to the charity.

The Inland Revenue has agreed that any payments under this agreement can be treated as royalty payments as long as the payments are made under a legal obligation, paid annually and are pure income profit. The last condition means that there must be no reciprocal services provided. The payments are therefore similar to covenanted donations. In a similar way the bank or finance company must deduct tax from the payments and pay them net to the charity, but the charity may recover the tax.

Arrangements of this type will apply to all fundraising mechanisms where the charity is entering into arrangements with companies for mutual benefit. Good legal advice should be obtained on the appropriate sort of licence agreement for the use of the charity's name and exactly how this should be structured for the charity.

Summary

Charities with many creative fundraising ideas will need to be alert to the tax implications of their efforts. Good communication between fundraisers and the financial management is essential to ensure that clearance for the new activity is obtained before it begins. It is often impossible to arrange matters to be tax-effective after the event, whereas considerable benefits may accrue to the charity if events are well-planned in advance and the available reliefs used properly.

Chapter 10

VAT

INTRODUCTION

VAT is a sales tax charged by businesses on the goods and services they supply, except for very small businesses whose turnover is below the VAT threshold. This has been £55,000 since 25 April 2002 and is subject to upward review each year, usually by an amount close to £1,000, although occasionally the Government of the day decides that they need a larger increase to help small business or to cope with inflation. Whilst many charities have gross income exceeding the VAT threshold, many of them are not registered for VAT.

It is also widely assumed that charities are exempt from paying VAT as part of the tax reliefs available to charities. This is far from the case and VAT actually costs charities millions of pounds each year, because they pay VAT when they purchase goods and services, just as ordinary individuals do.

Assessing the status of your organisation

The reason why charities are often not registered for VAT is that they are not undertaking business activities. If they are not registered for VAT, then they may not charge VAT, nor may they recover VAT on VATable goods and services they have purchased. Activities such as collecting donations or undertaking grant-funded work will always be non-business activities and therefore outside the scope of VAT.

On the other hand, charities frequently undertake activities which do fall within the scope of VAT, although some business activities are exempt from VAT, and some may be zero-rated, so VAT will not be chargeable on all business income.

A certain amount of planning can be done before an activity begins to arrange things to the benefit of the charity. The VAT rules are not, however, flexible and care must be taken. If in doubt, you should always contact your local VAT office to obtain a ruling for your specific situation.

Note that only VAT registered traders may recover VAT, and then only on purchases related to their business activities.

Glossary of VAT Terminology

Business Activities
Defined by VAT law as the exchange of goods or services for value.

Non-business Activities
Supplies made with no commercial intent, such as voluntary donations

Outside the Scope
Certain activities are not covered by the VAT regime, principally employment (salaries are not subject to VAT) and non-business transactions.

Exempt
Certain business activities do not carry any VAT because they are on a list of exempt goods or services, e.g. health services.

Taxable
The two categories of zero-rated and standard-rated come under a group of taxable activities.

Zero-rated
Certain business activities are taxable, but carry VAT at zero-rate.

Standard-rated
VAT must be charged by VAT-registered businesses at 17.5%.

Input VAT
The VAT on business purchases which may be recovered by offsetting against output VAT.

Output VAT
The VAT you charge on sales and which you have to collect from customers. You then pay this over to H M Customs and Excise (after deducting input VAT you have paid out on purchases).

REGISTERING FOR VAT

To register for VAT, you must complete form VAT 1 available from the local VAT office (check the telephone directory under 'Customs and Excise'). You must also obtain a VAT registration number which must then be quoted on all sales invoices.

Compulsory Registration

A business must register for VAT when it exceeds the VAT threshold. This is measured on a rolling twelve-month period, so that at the end of any month if you look back over the previous year and income from taxable business activities exceeds the threshold (£55,000 since 25 April 2002) you should register for VAT. You have a month to obtain and complete the form. You must quote your VAT registration number on all invoices. Note that VAT cannot be charged retrospectively – the VAT threshold is simply a trigger for registration and only once you are registered do you start charging VAT. However, you may recover some VAT on purchases (input VAT) incurred prior to registration; this would include purchases of goods up to one year prior to registration and services up to six months prior to registration. However, these would have to be purchases for business activity (see p165 – VAT recovery).

You should register for VAT if you see that you will exceed the threshold in the next 30 days. Registration is also possible for new enterprises where it is likely that they will have to register compulsorily at a later date. You may have to give evidence of contracts or business plans to support your case for registration from the point that the business is established. Since you will usually be claiming back VAT on setting up costs, H M Customs and Excise will retain the right to claw back VAT paid to the business if turnover does not exceed the registration threshold by the end of the first year.

Voluntary Registration

You may also register for VAT even if your taxable supplies are below the threshold, although you must have some taxable supplies. Registration is advantageous because you can recover VAT on purchases relating to the taxable activity. You will need to consider carefully who will be paying the VAT – remember it is the end consumer who ultimately pays – so to register for VAT and start charging VAT on admission fees for example, would effectively be an increase in the admission price for the ordinary public.

VAT – Categories of Supplies

In order to establish whether the charity should register for VAT or not, one needs to go through the sources of income and identify the VAT category they belong to.

◆ Non-business
◆ Exempt
◆ Taxable, further sub-divided into:
  Zero-rated
  Standard-rated

Non-Business Supplies

These will usually be one-way transactions where something is given without expectation of something in return. Voluntary donations and grants to the charity therefore come into this category. So will welfare activities, where the contribution paid by a beneficiary is minimal. The rule is that the charity should be subsidising the activity by at least 15% of the total cost. Many centres providing meals and drinks where a small charge is made will come into this category, as they receive grants and donations to subsidise the service. Non-business supplies are not subject to VAT and do not count towards the registration threshold.

Exempt Supplies

These are all activities that are specified as exempt by VAT legislation and include broad categories such as health and education, therefore including many of the activities of charities. The following activities will be exempt for VAT purposes:

◆ medical care by recognised professionals
◆ education in schools, universities, colleges (fees, not equipment)
◆ vocational training courses run by eligible bodies, including charities and some other not for profit bodies (vocational meaning that the training should help people in their work or voluntary work and can include educational conferences)
◆ nursing homes, registered care homes, hospices
◆ registered nurseries, creches and playgroups
◆ activities of youth clubs
◆ renting out residential accommodation
◆ welfare services provided on a not-for-profit basis by charities
◆ fundraising events run by charities or their trading subsidiary.

There are further specific exemptions for certain activities and the above list is not exhaustive. Fundraising events are covered in more detail later in this chapter.

Exempt supplies are not subject to VAT and do not count towards the registration threshold.

Zero-rated Supplies

Some activities are taxable, but at zero rate. These are listed in a schedule to the VAT legislation, which is amended from time to time. There are some broad areas which apply to everyone, such as food. The following activities are zero-rated supplies:

◆ sale of publications, including magazines and newsletters
◆ sale of children's clothes and shoes
◆ sale of food (not takeaways)
◆ exports.

There are also some activities that are zero-rated when undertaken by charities, such as sales of donated goods by a charity or its subsidiary.

The turnover on these activities will count towards the VAT threshold when considering the need for registration. It also means that charities with some of these activities can voluntarily register for VAT.

Standard-rated Supplies

Most sales of goods and services will be standard-rated, even if they are supplied by a charity. This includes many fundraising activities that involve merchandising or sales of some sort. It is safest to assume that an activity will be standard-rated unless you can establish that it is non-business, exempt or zero-rated.

The income from sales of standard-rated and zero-rated supplies together counts towards the threshold for VAT registration. Voluntary registration will be an option for charities with some standard-rated supplies who do not exceed the threshold, although this would mean that they would have to charge VAT on the standard-rated activity.

VAT Categories for Certain Activities

Some of the activities undertaken by charities need further consideration in order to establish their VAT category.

Membership Subscriptions

Many charities operate a membership subscription system both as a means of fundraising and of building awareness of the objects of the charity. Membership schemes where the membership benefits are limited to voting rights and the receipt of an annual report will be treated as exempt for the purposes of VAT.

However, where the member receives any other benefits, such as a quarterly magazine or reduced admission fees, the subscription will be deemed to be a payment for which something is received and will include VAT at the full rate, unless you agree an apportionment with Customs and Excise.

Apportionment means that you attribute certain values to the various membership benefits, by reference to cost or the price non-members pay. Then the VAT category applicable to the goods and services provided as membership benefits determines the VAT rate to apply. This must be agreed with the local VAT office in advance.

Example – Membership Subscriptions

Membership benefits amount to a free magazine four times a year (normal cost £2.50 to non-members) and a discount on tickets for performances worth approximately £2 per ticket. The overall discounts given last year according to the accounting records totalled £24,000. Since there are 3,000 members, this is the equivalent of each member benefiting from discounts of £8 each in a year. The membership subscription is £35 per year. The apportionment could be calculated as follows:

Magazine	£10	Zero-rated benefit
Discount on tickets	£ 8	Standard-rated benefit
Balance = Donation	£17	Outside the scope

The optimum position is achieved by increasing the zero-rated element of a subscription. This means that all input VAT relating to membership can be recovered, whilst the output VAT is zero.
(See Chapter 11 for notes on the interaction between VAT and gift aid on membership.)

Sponsorship

There is a significant difference between a corporate donation and corporate sponsorship. If a donation is received, then nothing should be given to the company in return. Sponsorship, on the other hand, is a reciprocal arrangement. The company receives advertising or promotional services in return for the cash given to the charity. Sponsorship is therefore a business arrangement and is standard-rated. It is also potentially liable to corporation tax because it is trading income. Consequently, some advance planning is needed for this type of fundraising and most charities set up a separate trading company for this and other business income. The trading company is usually registered for VAT right from the beginning.

Alternatively, the company could give a donation to the charity, possibly under gift aid and receive no benefits in return. The charity may simply acknowledge the gift in the annual report and this would be outside the scope of VAT.

Sponsorship received for an exempt fundraising event will be covered by the exemption and no VAT is payable in those circumstances.

Admission Charges

Admission charges are standard-rated. If you charge for entrance to exhibitions, museums, visitors' centres or any premises or events then this will be standard-rated and you will have to charge VAT if your organisation goes over the VAT threshold and registers for VAT. There is, however, some scope for keeping the standard-rated element to the basic charge only and inviting donations over and above the basic charge. You should not rig the charges though, and the basic charge should be sufficient to cover the costs. You may decide not to charge for entrance at all and invite donations only, but you must allow anyone to enter, regardless of their contribution or lack of it, otherwise the donation is no longer truly voluntary.

Fundraising Events

Fundraising events organised by charities (or their trading subsidiary where the profits are passed up to the charity) are exempt from VAT. This means that you do not charge VAT on the entrance fee to an annual fete (as an example), but note that generally no input VAT may be recovered either. The exemption can be applied to annual events, and charities may have 15 events of the same kind in the same location in one financial year. Events may be held by the charity or its training subsidiary, but the limit of 15 would apply to them jointly. You may have different types of events and each one may qualify for the exemption. The exemption will apply to all supplies at the event, even sponsorship and the sale of tee-shirts, mugs, and other goods. Events can be widely interpreted, so that it can include an event on the internet and it does include participatory events such as golf days.

Events do not have to be organised with a clear fundraising purpose, which should be made known to the public. Any events which create a distortion of competition and place a commercial enterprise at a disadvantage will not be exempt fundraising events. Events where more than two days accommodation is provided do not fall with the exemption.

Small-scale events can be ignored, as long as the aggregate gross takings from events of that type in that location do not exceed £1,000 in a week. This means that jumble sales and coffee mornings are not included when counting up the number of events.

VAT Recovery

VAT on purchases can only be recovered by businesses registered for VAT. For ordinary businesses and the trading subsidiaries of charities, this is straightforward and all input VAT is recovered. For charities, it is frequently not so simple, as they have income that falls into several different VAT categories. Most charities will have some donations or grants, and since these are non-business supplies, the recovery of VAT on purchases will be restricted.

Calculating Recoverable VAT

The first step is to directly relate purchases to the different areas of activity. This then gives the amount of VAT on purchases directly attributable to each category of VAT. The VAT on purchases which cannot be directly related to a particular area of activity, such as shared premises and administration costs, is known as non-attributable VAT. Under the standard method, a proportion of this input VAT will be recoverable, depending on the relative amount of taxable business income compared to the total income. Special methods can be agreed with the VAT office, using a different basis to calculate the proportion of non-attributable VAT to be recovered. The VAT office will consider any basis which will give a fair proportion and which can be checked by their officers. Options might include staff time spent on different activities or the amount of floor space taken up by different activities. You must have the agreement of the VAT office before you begin to use a special method.

Whether you use a special method or the standard method, you will need to recalculate your VAT recovery at the end of the tax year to calculate any annual adjustment necessary. For this purpose the tax year ends on 31 March, 30 April or 31 May, depending on your VAT quarters.

Partial Exemption Rules

The partial exemption rules may apply if the charity makes any exempt supplies as well as taxable supplies. (Note that if the charity only makes exempt supplies or only makes exempt and non-business supplies then it will not be allowed to register for VAT and therefore will not be able to recover any VAT.) The *de minimis* limits allow charities with low amounts of input VAT attributable to exempt activity to recover this VAT. Currently, (May 2002) the *de minimis* limit is £625 per month on average (£7,500 a year) and not more than 50% of total input VAT. The percentage test is to ensure that the exempt activity is a minor part of the organisation's activity as a whole. Note that the term input VAT means the VAT on business purchases in VAT law, so the VAT on purchases relating to non-business activity is not strictly input VAT. Therefore, when undertaking the partial exemption calculations, the 50% test should be applied to business input VAT only.

Organisations with exempt activity need to check the de minimis limit every time they prepare a VAT return and they also have to undertake an annual adjustment. This means a recalculation of the figures on an annual basis, to deal with any distortions produced by seasonal variations.

EXAMPLE VAT RECOVERY - ANNUAL CALCULATION

Income	VAT Category	£	% of total income
Grants	Outside the scope	500,000	
Donations	Outside the scope	200,000	
Investment Income	Outside the scope	50,000	
(Sub total)	*Outside the scope*	*750,000*	87%
Sales of Publications	Zero-rated	50,000	6%
Rental Income	Exempt	50,000	6%
Management Charges	Standard-rated	10,000	1%
Total Income		**860,000**	

VAT on Purchases	£	VAT Recovery
Directly Attributable to Publications	1,750	Recover 100%
Directly Attributable to Rental Income	1,400	Partial exemption
Shared Costs:Non-Attributable VAT	7,070	Recover same %
Total	**10,220**	

Spreading Non-Attributable VAT	% of total income	£	VAT Recovery
Outside the scope	87%	6,151	
Zero-rated	6%	424	Recover 100%
Exempt	6%	424	
Standard-rated	1%	71	Recover 100%
Total		**7,070**	

Partial Exemption Check	£
Directly Attributable to Rental Income	1,400
% of Non-Attributable Relating to Exempt	424
Total	**1,824**

This is below the *de minimis* level of £7,500 per year, but we need to check that the exempt input VAT is less than 50% of total input VAT. Total input VAT is £10,220, less £6,151 relating to outside the scope = £4,069 business input VAT. 50% of this is £2,034. Yes, the exempt input VAT of £1,824 is less than 50% of total input VAT of £2,034.

Recoverable VAT	£
Directly attributable to publications	1,750
Non-attributable- zero rate	424
Non-attributable- standard rate	71
Directly attributable to rental income	1,400
Non-attributable- exempt	424
A. Total	**4,069**
B. Irrecoverable VAT (outside the scope)	**£6,151**
Total VAT paid (A+B)	**£10,220**

Recoverable VAT is £4,069 which is approximately 40% of the total VAT paid

The overall recovery rate is therefore approximately 40%.

Improving VAT Recovery

The options available for individual charities will vary enormously, as much will depend on the nature of the activities and the balance of these between different categories of VAT. There are however a few general rules to consider.

◆ Relate purchases to particular activities as far as possible, because VAT on purchases relating to taxable activities will be 100% recoverable.

◆ Make use of the partial exemption de minimis rule if possible. Remember fundraising events are exempt even when organised through the trading subsidiary. Both the charity and the trading subsidiary can maximise benefit from these rules.

◆ Increase the proportion of business activities, so that the formula for calculating recoverable VAT on the non-attributable input VAT is more favourable.

◆ Use a special method, which should be agreed with Customs and Excise in advance, for calculating the recovery rate on non-attributable VAT.

◆ Maximise zero-rated supplies, rather than non-business ones. For example, subscriptions where the benefits to members are printed matter can be counted as zero-rated, by agreement with the VAT office. Zero-rated income allows you to recover the related input VAT and increases the taxable proportion of total income, thus improving the proportion of non-attributable VAT to recover. Charity shops selling donated goods should be kept within the charity for this reason, unless you have a group registration.

◆ Consider group registration if the charity has a trading subsidiary. This will mean that the total supplies of the whole group are the basis of the apportionment for calculating the recoverable part of non-attributable input VAT. If the trading subsidiary has significant taxable supplies, then the recovery rate will be greatly enhanced.

Zero-rating Reliefs

There is quite a long list of items which can be supplied at zero-rate VAT when supplied to a charity, although most are for medical supplies and aids for disabled people. To obtain the zero-rating, the charity supplies a certificate to the supplier, stating that the purchase qualifies for zero-rating. An example of the certificate is given in the relevant VAT leaflet, which is essential reading for charities working in the medical or disability field. This is a valuable relief to charities, since it is a direct cost saving and available to VAT registered and unregistered charities alike. Examples of some of the items which should qualify for zero-rating when purchased by a charity are:

◆ building work to give access to charity-run buildings for the disabled

◆ special adaptation of toilets and bathrooms for the disabled

- advertisements of any type for any purpose on any media. This does not include the purchase of the media itself, nor does it include the development of charity websites for their own use
- preparation and design of advertisements
- collecting tins of any description, providing they are indelibly marked and capable of sealing
- specially adapted equipment for use by a disabled person
- ambulances
- lifeboats and rescue equipment
- minibuses for transporting disabled people (when purchased by a charity which provides care for those people)
- talking books for the blind
- medical equipment if purchased out of donated funds.

The conditions for the zero-rating are quite specific and must be adhered to carefully. The onus is on the charity to only provide a certificate for zero-rating to a supplier when it is appropriate. The charity is potentially liable to make good the VAT in the event of error.

Property Transactions and VAT

The rules on property transactions are very complex and it is wise to seek professional advice. This may prove worthwhile, as the sums involved will be significant.

As a general rule, VAT will always be charged on building repairs, extensions, improvements, refurbishment, alterations and so on. Only new construction of separate buildings may be zero-rated if it will be used for residential purposes or by a charity for its non-business activity. Substantial alterations (those requiring approval) to listed buildings may qualify for zero-rating also, providing the building will be used for non-business purposes by a charity.

If you are planning extensive building works, then it is worth considering your VAT position as a whole. The VAT on building costs is recoverable by businesses, unless a large proportion of their income is exempt.

VAT Planning

There is some scope for planning activities to be advantageous from a VAT point of view. The scope is somewhat limited, however, as in some matters you have no choice. Care is needed and professional advice should be sought. The penalties for misdemeanours and even errors are quite severe.

Avoiding Registration

Remember, a whole organisation has to register for VAT, although a separate trading company is a separate legal entity and therefore registers for VAT in its own right if necessary. You must look at all activities of an entity to check whether the threshold is exceeded. If you channel certain trading activities into the trading company, then it may be possible to keep the charity below the threshold or entirely outside the scope. Consider the following options:

◆ raise donations rather than sponsorships
◆ ask for donations rather than charge entrance fees
◆ keep subscriptions largely outside the scope
◆ fundraise through one-off fundraising events
◆ obtain sponsorship for one-off fundraising events rather than for regular activities, as it is then included in the exemption.

You may apply for exemption from registration if the majority of your taxable supplies are zero-rated. In order to be exempt from registration, you need to be able to show that you would also be in a repayment situation. In other words, you would always be entitled to recover more VAT than you would be liable to pay over.

Achieving Registration

In order to register for VAT, you must have some taxable supplies. You cannot even register voluntarily if you only have non-business and exempt income. Consider:

◆ charging for entrance to exhibitions, events and so on
◆ charging for publications (zero-rated)
◆ providing benefits to members in return for their subscription
◆ changing fundraising events into regular events
◆ charging a fee to companies for sponsorship or advertising
◆ charging to the trading company for services.

Be careful that you do not end up trading in the charity so that a tax liability is incurred. Regular fundraising events and commercial sponsorship would be trading and unlikely to be primary purpose trading, so potentially taxable. (The profits would be taxable, so if you did find yourself in this predicament, you would identify costs relating to the income as far as possible to reduce the taxable profits.)

Minimising VAT

This is worth consideration by VAT registered and unregistered organisations alike.

◆ Use zero-rating reliefs as much as possible.
◆ Buy from other charities or suppliers not registered for VAT.
◆ Obtain printed matter at zero-rates and ensure that all associated work is handled through the printer so that the whole supply is zero-rated.
◆ Plan building works carefully and obtain at zero-rates if possible.
◆ Use venues run by educational charities for training and conferences as they will be able to exempt the charge.

Summary

VAT legislation is complex and subject to regular change and amendment as new cases go to court and European legislation affects UK law. Care needs to be taken in this area and proper advice sought from a specialist. This chapter is brief and does not cover all aspects in detail, so look at the reference materials for further information if you consider that a particular aspect may apply to your organisation. If you are uncertain about the status of a particular activity or your VAT position, then it is wise to obtain a ruling from your local VAT office.

Chapter 11

TAX-EFFECTIVE GIVING

Charities can benefit from their tax exempt status to receive donations gross of tax or to reclaim tax that has been paid on the money donated. The range of tax reliefs on charitable giving has been expanded over recent years, such that this is now a considerable help to charities receiving voluntary income from individuals and companies.

The main forms of charitable giving that are eligible for tax relief are:

◆ gift aid
◆ payroll giving
◆ gifts of shares and property
◆ gifts in kind

Note that the Government department dealing with all questions and claims in relation to tax effective giving is a specialist unit within the Inland Revenue, referred to as IR Charities. Details of how to contact them may be found in Useful Addresses.

GIFT AID

This is the principal method by which charities encourage donors to make their donations tax effective. Since April 2000, gift aid can apply to any amount and can apply to regular giving as well as one-off donations. Gift aid can only apply to cash donations, and it should not be used for the purchase of goods or services. Thus, the purchase of raffle tickets or tickets to fundraising events will not come within gift aid. New rules apply to the level of benefit donors may receive whilst still giving under gift aid rules (see below).

Benefits Rules on Gift Aid

Some benefits are allowed despite the general rule that the donation should be a pure gift. There is a sliding scale of allowable benefit depending on the level of donation. The old rule for covenants which allowed heritage charities to disregard free admission to sites when considering the value of benefits has been retained and extended to gift aid.

Total donations in the tax year	Total value of benefits in the tax year
£0 - £100	25%
£101-£1,000	£25
£1,001 +	2.5%

The absolute maximum value of benefits in a tax year is £250. These limits apply separately to each donation, but you also have to review the total amount received from a donor over a whole tax year. It is therefore possible that you will have treated gifts received early in the year as gift aid donations, but that the accumulation of donations and benefits leads to elimination of donations from that individual or company from gift aid. Note that the benefit rules apply to companies and individuals alike.

Benefits provided to a member of the donor's family will also be caught under these rules. The definition of family in this context includes a spouse, children and grandchildren, parents or grandparents and siblings, as well as their spouses. In addition, benefits may not be provided to a company owned by the donor.

Membership Subscriptions

Membership subscriptions may be donated under gift aid, providing the benefits provided under the membership scheme fall within the limits above. The Inland Revenue disregard annual reports, newsletters, magazines, members' handbooks and programmes of events providing further information about the charity's work when considering what constitutes a benefit. Free admission to events or reduced prices do count as benefits and need to be valued.

Sometimes charities secure discounts for their members from outside suppliers. These discounts will count as benefits if they are received as a result of the membership subscription.

The rules for gift aid are not those for VAT, and it is quite possible that a charity would have to calculate an apportionment of benefits for VAT purposes, even though they are benefits that are allowed or disregarded for gift aid purposes.

Valuation of Benefits

A mere acknowledgement will not count as a benefit and does not need to be valued. Companies making donations to charity under gift aid may not receive free promotion or advertising as a result of their donation, so this precludes the prominent display of their logo on charity literature or website.

The usual basis for valuing a benefit is to look for the price that would be paid in a commercial setting by a third party. This may be the cover price on a magazine or book, or the normal ticket price for an event. Where there is no comparison to the commercial value of the goods or service, then the charity has to assess the value to the recipient. It may be necessary to calculate the benefit by reference to the cost to the charity where there is no external comparison. For example, a charity should calculate the per head cost for an event that is not open to the public.

Information about the charity's work contained in newsletters, bulletins, magazines and journals will be accepted as having nil value under these rules. This will be the case even if the publication has a cover price. Note that the information does have to be relevant to the charity's objects and educate readers or promote the work of the charity.

Where the benefit is a discount or a reduced price, it may be difficult to calculate the value to the donor because the level of take up will determine the total value of the benefit. In these circumstances, the Inland Revenue will accept a calculation based on the overall level of take up to assess the value of the discount.

Example

As a membership benefit, members may attend training courses organised by the charity at half price. New members attend far more courses and take advantage of the discount to a greater extent than members of several years. The total value of the benefit to all members in a year can be ascertained from the record of attendance at training courses. The total value of benefits is then divided by the total number of members to calculate the value of this benefit per member.

Care is needed when benefits such as discounts may be spread over a period of time of less than 12 months, as there may then be a need to annualise the benefit and the donation received.

Example

A single payment of £100 to a theatre gives the donor the right to 10% discount on theatre tickets purchased in the next six months, valued at £24. On the face of it, this is within the benefit limits set out in the table above. However, annualising applies to both the donation and the benefit because the benefits are for a period of less than 12 months. So their annual value is double these amounts for the purpose of checking the benefit limits. Thus the annualised figures are £200 for the donation and £48 for the benefits. Thus, the value of the benefits exceeds £25 and gift aid may not apply. Had the scheme been amended so that the period for the discount was one year, then annualising would not apply.

Gift Aid for Individuals

Only UK taxpayers may make donations under gift aid, but the tax paid may be income tax or capital gains tax. Even though the charity may reclaim tax at basic rate, it is sufficient if the individual has at least paid tax at the lower rate. Members of the armed forces and government serving overseas and non-resident UK taxpayers may make donations under gift aid.

Charities are encouraged to remind regular donors to inform the charity if their tax status changes.

Declarations

Individuals have to give the charity a declaration confirming certain information. The declaration may be given before or after the donation, and may cover a single donation, a series of donations or all donations from that individual. Declarations should cover the following;

◆ The name and address of the donor
◆ The name of the charity
◆ A description of the donations to which the declaration relates
◆ A declaration that the donations are to be treated as gift aid donations

Written declarations should also include a note explaining that the donation must come out of income on which tax has been paid.

EXAMPLE
GIFT AID DECLARATION

Note that this example contains a space for signature and date – these are not required by law, but they may be useful to prove that the individual did provide the declaration and necessary if they are declaring that all donations from the date of the declaration will be gift aid donations.

You may add further information for your own purposes, such as a direct debit mandate. You may also simplify the declaration if you are incorporating it into a particular form where there is only one option and the gift aid will apply only to that donation.

NAME OF CHARITY

DONOR DETAILS

Title   First name   Surname

Address

              Postcode

DETAILS OF DONATION

I want the charity to treat

 * the enclosed donation of £_____

 * all donations I make under the direct debit mandate below

 * the donations I make on or after the date of this declaration until I notify you otherwise

as Gift Aid donations

*delete as appropriate

Signature   Date

Note that:

◆ You should be paying income tax or capital gains tax as this declaration means that the charity will be reclaiming the tax you have paid and adding it to the value of your donation.

◆ You can claim higher rate tax relief on this donation by entering the amount of the donation on your tax return.

◆ You should notify us if your circumstances change and you are no longer a taxpayer. We will no longer reclaim the tax on your donations.

Please notify us if your personal details such as name or address change so that we can update our records.

Telephone Declarations

Oral declarations can be given, for example over the telephone. In this case, the charity must send a written record of the declaration. This should include the basic information above such as name, address, charity name and declaration that it is a gift aid donation. Additionally the written record should include the note about donations coming out of taxed income. Extra information for the written record is:

♦ A note explaining the donor's entitlement to cancel the declaration
♦ The date on which the donor gave the declaration to the charity
♦ The date on which the charity sent the written record to the donor.

An oral declaration is only valid if the charity has sent a written declaration. Donors can cancel their declaration at any time, but additionally with oral declarations they can cancel the declaration retrospectively if they do so within 30 days from the date of sending the written record.

Written records of oral declarations may be generated and retained by electronic means, with the written record being sent to the donor by email, for example. The system will need to be set up in such a way that an Inland Revenue audit will still be able to verify that that the written record has been sent to the donor.

Joint Declarations and Partnerships

Couples may make a joint declaration, but the declaration needs to identify how much is coming from each individual. Also they must each keep records for their own tax records. In England and Wales, the partners in a partnership much each agree to a declaration being made on their behalf and there has to be the power to do so in the partnership agreement. A donation has to be treated as being made by the individual partners. In Scotland a partnership is treated as a separate legal entity and one partner can make the declaration on behalf of the partnership.

Sponsored Events

Donations raised through sponsorship of individuals in an event are donations from the third party to the charity. It is not possible for the individual participant to collect the cash from sponsors and then make one gift aid donation of that money to the charity. However, it is possible to collect gift aid declarations from the individual sponsors. This can be achieved on one form that is both a sponsorship form and a declaration. The suggested format is for the gift aid declaration for a one-off donation to be printed at the top of the sponsorship sheet, with individual donors able to opt in by ticking a box. The information gathered on the form must include the sponsor's name and home address, including postcode, and the amount actually collected. It may be necessary to record the date collected and the date the money as actually handed over to the charity. It has to be possible to trace the amounts entered in the charity's own books back to individual donors and their declarations.

Gifts of Foreign Currency

Gifts of foreign currency notes and coins to charities are eligible for gift aid. Guidance from the Inland Revenue has confirmed that gift aid can be claimed in the same way as any other donation. Declarations will be needed from donors, and records maintained in the same way as any other donation. You need to keep records of the amounts donated in each currency and the sterling value should be calculated on the date of the donation.

Higher Rate Relief

Individuals may claim relief from higher rate tax by entering the gift aid donation on their tax return. The relief given is the difference between basic rate and higher rates of tax. For example, a donor makes a gift of £10. The charity can recover basic rate tax relief on this of £2.82 (£10 x 22/78 where basic rate tax is 22%). This makes the gross gift £12.82 and the difference between basic rate relief and higher rate relief is £2.31 (18% of £12.82).

From April 2003, taxpayers will be able to carry back the higher rate element of gift aid relief to the previous tax year. In addition, taxpayers will be able to nominate a charity to receive all or part of a tax repayment that is due to them.

Record Keeping

The gift aid rules do require the retention of all written declarations received and copies of the written records sent to donors who have made a telephone declaration. You need to be able to link the declaration to the donations made by that particular donor. Charities will therefore need to think through a system that will achieve this, perhaps through reference numbers. It also means that declarations made for all future donations will need to be kept for a very long time. You may need to consider whether you will have a system of refreshing these on a regular basis.

Claims

Claims for repayment of income tax have to be submitted to the Inland Revenue on forms R68 (2000) and accompanying schedules. In particular, charities must complete the supplementary pages R68 (New Gift Aid) where the details of all gift aid donations have to be listed. There is a substitute schedule available for claims relating to gift aid arising from sponsored events. IR Charities also recommends that a separate claim be made for this type of gift aid to make the claim more straightforward. If it is a very large event, then prior notice should be given to IR Charities.

Before making their first claim, charities need to register with IR Charities, and may be asked to submit their governing instrument and last audited accounts to validate their entitlement to reclaim tax on donations. Claims may then be made as frequently as the charity wishes. Claims should relate to only one tax year, however. Charities may substitute their own forms, but this should be agreed with IR Charities in advance. This may be appropriate for charities using computer software to generate claims.

Charities will only be reclaiming tax paid by individuals, as companies no longer deduct tax from gift aid donations to charities.

Claims may also include income tax deducted at source from interest on bank and building society accounts (if not receiving this gross), royalties and other types of annual payment.

Gift Aid Audits

The Inland Revenue do undertake regular audits of charities making substantial gift aids claims. In particular, they are looking for declarations to support the gift aid claims for individuals. They will attempt to trace an amount shown on a gift aid claim to the cash records, bank statements and the individual donor record showing the declaration. If an amount has been improperly claimed, then this has to be paid back to the Inland Revenue.

They are also likely to check the level of benefits given to individuals and companies to ensure that these are within the allowable limits.

Company Donations

Companies no longer have to deduct basic rate tax from donations, as was the case before April 2000. Companies therefore pay donations gross of tax to charities and have to include them in their corporation tax computation and corporation tax return to obtain tax relief. The rules on benefits apply to companies, and companies may not use a gift aid donation to purchase goods or services from a charity.

Deeds of Covenant

After April 2000, tax relief for donations under deeds of covenant come within the gift aid scheme and there is no separate relief for these donations. This means that gift aid forms have to be used and the same conditions apply. As a transitional measure, current donors with deeds of covenant will not have to complete new gift aid declarations.

PAYROLL GIVING

Individuals may give to a nominated charity by direct deduction from their pay. This may apply to pensioners as well as those in employment. The scheme has to be operated by the employer, who deducts the donation from gross pay before calculating the tax due, in a similar way to pension deductions. The employer then sends the amount of the donation to an intermediary or payroll giving agent. Agents are generally consortia of charities and are charities themselves. They are approved by Inland Revenue Charities. The agent collates the amounts sent from different employers and distributes them to the charities nominated by the employees.

There is no minimum or maximum on the amount that can be given in this way. Donors may not benefit in any way and should receive nothing in return for their donation. They may receive items of nominal value and information abut the work of the charity. In order to promote the scheme, the Government is paying a 10% supplement to the recipient charities in the period from April 2000 to April 2003. The supplement is claimed by the payroll giving agencies and distributed by them to the charities, together with the donations made under payroll giving. Agencies must distribute funds to charities within 60 days of receipt from the employer.

Agencies may charge an amount for administration and this is usually deducted from the amount distributed to the charity.

GIFTS OF SHARES AND PROPERTY

Since April 2000, individuals and companies can get tax relief on shares donated to charities. Qualifying shares and securities are:

◆ shares and securities listed or dealt on the UK stock exchange, including the Alternative Investment Market (AIM)
◆ shares and securities listed or dealt in on recognised foreign stock exchanges (see list published by IR Charities as an appendix to leaflet IR178 and on the Inland Revenue website)
◆ units in an authorised unit trust
◆ shares in an open-ended investment company
◆ holdings in certain foreign collective investment scheme.

Where there is any doubt as to whether the shares qualify, then advice should be sought from IR Charities.

The amount of relief is calculated as:

◆ the market value of the shares at the date of disposal
◆ plus the transaction costs, such as broker's fees
◆ less any amounts or benefits received from the charity as a result of the gift of shares.

The date of disposal will normally be the date the stock transfer form is signed.

Individuals show this amount as a deduction from taxable income on their tax return. The value of the tax relief is therefore dependent on whether they are a higher rate taxpayer or not, as relief will be given at the marginal rate of tax. In addition, the individual does not include the disposal of the shares when calculating capital gains for the year. The charity does not reclaim any tax on this form of gift.

Companies may give shares they hold as investments, but not shares in their own company. They may be given or sold at less than market value. Relief is given to companies by allowing the amount as a deduction against company profits for corporation tax purposes. The disposal of the shares is excluded from any chargeable gains calculations.

Gifts of property to charities

Since April 2002, individuals and companies wishing to give property to charities can now do so under similar rules to the gift of shares.

GIFTS IN KIND

This principally applies to businesses wishing to support charities, and can include sole traders, partnerships and companies. There a number of ways in which businesses may wish to give. Gifts in kind do not qualify for gift aid, but instead the business may claim relief by deducting the relevant amount from their taxable profits.

◆ Donated equipment or trading stock must be an article manufactured or sold in the course of the trade, or equipment used in the course of the trade. In this case, no action is needed, but relief is given by a relaxation of the normal rules which require the inclusion of the market value as a deemed disposal. Donated fixed assets should be included in the capital allowances calculation at nil proceeds.
◆ The secondment of an employee to work for a charity on a temporary basis qualifies for relief, which is given by allowing the total employment costs as a tax deductible expense.

INDEX

FURTHER READING

Most of the organisations listed under useful addresses produce guidance notes and publications which are worth obtaining. Other titles by Kate Sayer in the **Practical Guide** *series, published by the Directory of Social Change in association with Sayer Vincent Chartered Accountants*

A Practical Guide to Charity Accounting, 1st edition, available in 2003.

A Practical Guide to VAT, 2nd edition, 2001, £12.95

Finance

The Charities Manual (Tolley's, published every 3-4 months) £40.00

The Charity Treasurer's Handbook, Gareth G Morgan, DSC, 1st edition, 2002, £9.95

Financial Stewardship of Charities, Adrian Poffley, DSC, 1st edition, 2002, £19.95

In addition, the magazine NGO Finance covers all issues concerning finance and funding as they affect the charity sector. This is a useful source of up-to-date information and it appears ten times a year. (Contact: Plaza Publishing, 1A Tradescant Road, SW4.)

Tax and Trading

Charities and Taxation, Adrian Randall and Stephen Williams (ICSA, 1st edition, 1995) £16.95

Craigmyle Guide to Charitable Giving and Taxation, Craigmyle Co (Craigmyle, 1996) £39.50

Tolley's VAT Guide, Bob Wareham (Tolley's, 1st edition, 1998) £79.90

Charity Law

The Voluntary Sector Legal Handbook, Sandy Adirondack & James Sinclair Taylor (DSC, 2nd edition, 2001)
Voluntary Organisations: £42.00; Others: £60.00.

Voluntary but not Amateur, Duncan Forbes, Ruth Hayes & Jacki Reason (London Voluntary Service Council, 6th edition, 2000) £22.95

Charity Law A-Z: Key Questions Answered, John Claricoat & Hilary Philips (Jordans, 2nd edition, 1998) £19.50

The Fundraiser's Guide to the Law, Bates, Wells & Braithwaite and Centre for Voluntary Sector Development (DSC, in association with CAF, 1st edition, 2000) £16.95

Investment

Investing Charity Funds, Michael Harbottle (Jordans, 1st edition, 1995) £37.50

Managing Charitable Investments, John Harrison (ICSA, 1st edition, 1994) £16.95

Management

Managing People, Gill Taylor & Christine Thomton (DSC, 1st edition, 1995) £10.95

Managing Recruitment and Selection, Gill Taylor (DSC, 1st edition, 1996) £11.50

Just About Managing, Sandy Adirondack (LVSC, 3rd edition, 1998) £18.95

Managing Without Profit, Mike Hudson (DSC, 2nd edition, 1999) £12.99

Essential Volunteer Management, Steve McCurley & Rick Lynch (DSC, 2nd edition, 1998) £14.95

The Health & Safety Handbook, Al Hinde & Charlie Kavanagh (DSC in Association with Liverpool Occupational Health Project, 2nd edition, 2001) £12.50

Databases

Fundraising Databases, Peter Flory (DSC in association with the Institute of Fundraising and CAF, 1st edition, 2001) £19.95

USEFUL ADDRESSES

Charity Commission for England and Wales

Central enquiry line, Tel: 0870 333 0123;
Website:www.charity-commission.gov.uk

Harmsworth House
13–15 Bouverie Street
London EC4Y 8DP
Fax: 020 7674 2300

2nd Floor, 20 King's Parade
Queen's Dock
Liverpool L3 4DQ
Fax: 0151 703 1555

Woodfield House
Tangier, Taunton
Somerset TA1 4BL
Fax: 01823 345003

Scotland
The Director
Scottish Charities Office
Crown Office
25 Chambers Street
Edinburgh EH1 1LA
Tel: 0131 226 2626
Fax: 0131 226 8912

Northern Ireland
Charities Branch
Department of Health and Social Services
C4.22, Castle Buildings
Stormont, Belfast BT4 3PP
Tel: 01232 522942/522780
Fax: 01232 522799

Inland Revenue

Charities Division (FICO)
St John's House
Merton Road
Bootle, Merseyside L69 9BB
Tel: 0151 472 6000

FICO Scotland
Trinity Park House
South Trinity Road
Edinburgh EH5 3SD
Tel: 0131 552 6255
Tax repayment claims: Tel: 0131 551 8127
Seeking charitable status: Tel: 0131 551 8802

H M Customs & Excise

Headquarters:
New King's Beam House
22 Upper Ground
London SE1 9PJ
Tel: 020 7620 1313

For VAT matters:
www.hmce.gov.uk

Companies House

Crown Way
Cardiff CF4 3UZ
Tel: 029 2038 0801

Charity Finance Directors' Group

87 Worship Street
London EC2A 2BE
Tel: 020 7247 2112
Fax: 020 7247 3113

Charities' Tax Reform Group

12 Little College Street
London SW1P 3SH
Tel: 020 7222 1265

National Council for Voluntary Organisations (NCVO)

Regent's Wharf
8 All Saints Street
London N1 9RL
Tel: 020 7713 6161
Fax: 020 7713 6300

Scottish Council for Voluntary Organisations (SCVO)

18–19 Claremont Crescent
Edinburgh EH7 4DQ
Tel: 0131 556 3882
Fax: 0131 556 0279

Wales Council for Voluntary Action (WCVA)

Baltic House
Mount Square
Cardiff CF10 5FH
Tel: 029 2043 1700
Fax: 029 2043 7701

Northern Ireland Council for Voluntary Action (NICVA)

127 Ormeau Road
Belfast BT7 1SH
Tel: 028 9032 1224
Fax: 028 9043 8350

Institute of Fundraising

5th Floor
Market Towers
1 Nine Elms Lane
London SW8 5NQ
Tel; 020 7627 3436
Fax: 020 7627 3508

The Charity Law Association

Paisner & Co.
Bouverie House
154 Fleet Street
London EC4A 2DQ
Tel: 020 7353 0299
Fax: 020 7583 8621

Association of Charitable Foundations

2 Plough Yard
Shoreditch High Street
London EC2A 3LP
Tel: 020 7422 8600
Fax: 020 7422 8606

National Association of Councils for Voluntary Service (NACVS)

3rd Floor
Arundel Court
177 Arundel Street
Sheffield S1 2NU
Tel: 0114 278 6636
Fax: 0114 278 7004
Website: www.nacvs.org.uk

ACEVO (Association of Chief Executives of Voluntary Organisations)

Middlesex House
130 College Road
Harrow
Middlesex HA1 1BQ
Tel: 0845 345 8481
Fax: 0845 345 8482

Charities Aid Foundation

Kings Hill
West Malling
Kent ME19 4TA
Tel: 01732 520000

Charity Investors' Group

DGAA-Homelife
1 Derry Street
London W8 5HY
Tel: 020 7396 6700
Fax: 020 396 6739

THE DIRECTORY OF SOCIAL CHANGE

The Directory of Social Change (DSC) is an independent voice for positive social change, set up in 1975 to help voluntary organisations become more effective. It does this by providing practical, challenging and affordable information and training to meet the current, emerging and future needs of the sector. DSC's main activities include:

◆ researching and publishing reference guides and handbooks;
◆ providing practical training courses;
◆ running conferences and briefing sessions;
◆ organising Charityfair, the biggest annual form for the sector;
◆ encouraging voluntary groups to network and share information;
◆ campaigning to promote the interests of the voluntary sector as a whole.

Titles published by DSC relevant to the subject of this book can be found in the Further Reading section. A free booklist can be obtained by mail order from the Publications Department. Telephone 020 7209 5151 or email books@dsc.org.uk, or visit the DSC website: www.dsc.org.uk. DSC also offers training courses in all aspects of financial management of charities. Contact addresses and telephone numbers for all departments can be found at the start of this book, opposite the Contents page.